FINDING
CANADIAN FACTS
FAST

FINDING
CANADIAN FACTS
FAST

Stephen Overbury

METHUEN

Toronto   New York   London   Sydney   Auckland

Canadian Cataloguing in Publication Data

Overbury, Stephen
   Finding Canadian facts fast

Bibliography: p.
Includes index.
ISBN 0-458-99150-3 (bound) 0-458-98250-4 (pbk.)

1. Research—Methodology—Handbooks, manuals,
etc. 2. Information services—Canada. 3. Canada—
Miscellanea. I. Title.

Q180.55.M4096 1985   001.4′2′0971   C85-098163-8

Cover design: Don Fernley

Printed and bound in Canada

  3 4 85 89 88 87 86

For Paul R., Frances G., and Jennifer.

CONTENTS

ACKNOWLEDGMENTS

This book would not have been written without the generous support and encouragement of many people. Salem Alaton, a reporter with the *Globe and Mail*, helped me immensely with editing and consulting services throughout the project.

Many other "information specialists" shared the secrets of their trade by consenting to long interviews and in so doing took the mystery out of research: John Zaritsky, a television producer with the Canadian Broadcasting Corporation; novelist Timothy Findley; Brian Land of the Ontario government's Legislative Library; Calvin Hill of the detective agency Intertel; David Mackenzie of the United Steelworkers of America; Gary S. Goodman of Goodman Communications Corporation of Glendale, California; Arthur R. Roberts of Atco Limited, Calgary; Frank Drea, a cabinet minister with the Ontario government; Professor J. M. S. Careless of the University of Toronto; Robert Reguly, an award-winning journalist based in Toronto; Julian Porter, a Toronto attorney; Dr. Louis Siminovitch of Toronto's Hospital for Sick Children; Kelly C. J. LaBrash of Canadian Protection Services Limited, Toronto; and Sean Fernando of A.B.C. Property and Lien Reports, Toronto.

My thanks to the following people for their help with the chapter on using libraries: Beryl L. Anderson of the Library Documentation Centre, National Library of Canada, and Susan Klement, an award-winning Toronto librarian.

I was assisted with the chapter on local government sources by: Michael John Smither of Municipal World Incorporated; Barbara G. Caplan of the City of Toronto Clerk's Department; Elizabeth Cuthbertson of the City of Toronto archives; Bruce Macnaughton of the Ontario Ministry of Municipal Affairs and Housing; and Bob Halifax of the City of Toronto Central Records Department.

I found the following people very helpful while I was researching provincial government sources: Allen Doppelt of the Ontario Ministry of Consumer and Commercial Relations; Irvin Lutsky of the

Investment Dealers' Association of Canada; Daniel Gordon, a Toronto attorney specializing in real estate law; Julian Sher, a Montreal-based journalist; Linda Stortz of Micromedia Limited; and Carl Vervoort of the Ontario Ministry of Transportation and Communications.

My thanks to these people for their assistance with federal government sources: Lorne J. Kenney and Nicole Lemay of the Industrial Relations Information Service of Labour Canada; Lionel Sauvé of the Canadian Government Publishing Centre in Ottawa; the staff at the Canada Service Bureaus; the staff at Consumer & Corporate Affairs Canada; Heather Mitchell, a Toronto attorney; Murray Rankin of the Faculty of Law, University of Victoria; Michael Dagg, a freelance researcher based in Ottawa; and Raulet Gaudet, an Ottawa-based journalist with Radio Canada International.

In preparing the chapter on court records, I was assisted by: Harold J. Levy of the Law Reform Commission of Canada, who is currently writing a book about access to court records; Stuart M. Robertson, an Ottawa attorney; James Moore of the federal Department of Justice; David A. Avery of the Ontario Ministry of the Attorney General; and Warren J. Dunlop of the Supreme Court of Ontario.

Other people who assisted me include: Michael Dufault, a Toronto-based freelance editor; Victor Brunka of SVP Canada Limited; the staff of the Archives of Labor and Urban Affairs at the Walter P. Reuther Library, Wayne State University (where, believe it or not, I obtained my background information on Frank Drea!); Donald Armitage of Dun and Bradstreet International; the Centre for Investigative Journalism at Carleton University; the staff of the Faculty of Library Science at the University of Toronto; and Anne-Marie Prendiville.

Colleen Daragh, my editor, and Stephanie Stone, my copy editor, were both helpful and a pleasure to work with. And I owe a special thanks to Methuen's trade editor, Greg Cable, for his encouragement.

Finally, the ideas in this book were developed by hundreds of people in many walks of life. I am referring to those people who attended my seminars and courses on research techniques and sources at the University of Toronto, Seneca College, Humber College, the Skills Exchange, the United Steelworkers of America, the United Auto Workers, the Ontario Public Service Employees Union, and the Amalgamated Transit Union.

Introduction

One rule I've learned as a researcher over the last 12 years is: There is no such thing as information you can't access. The "Information Age" is here to stay, and, like it or not, privacy is an endangered species. Reading this book will make that clear. Everyone can find almost any fact quickly with a little know-how and practice.

I first proposed teaching courses on the principles of research to various educational institutions two years ago, and I was surprised to learn that such courses were not offered anywhere except through some faculties of Library Science and Law and were thus available only to a minority of Canadians. This is ironic, because information gathering is a survival skill, as vital to our everyday functioning as reading itself.

Most of us do not research information at all. Rather, we rely on assumptions and guesswork to make decisions. Think back to the last time you purchased a faulty electrical appliance because you *assumed* it was a good buy—and later discovered that another, more reliable, product was available at considerably less cost. Or have you ever invested in the stock market without researching any companies—and lost money? Perhaps, during an interview with a prospective employer, you have been asked if you had any questions, and you've found yourself unable to utter a word because you weren't properly prepared—you assumed that *you* would be answering all the questions.

Speaking of faulty assumptions, here's a serious one I once made: It began with an anonymous tip from someone, claiming that a Canadian company was exporting tank engines to South Africa with the support of federal government funds. To a freelance journalist, this was potentially explosive material. On the surface it meant that Canada was violating the United Nations arms embargo against South Africa.

I began my research in the right manner. I contacted the company and, claiming I was writing a human-interest story about enterprising Canadian businesses, asked for a tour of their facilities. They agreed to this. On arriving, I saw a battered Centurion tank and hundreds of tank treads in the firm's yard. Inside a warehouse I noticed a blackboard with the words "South Africa" written on it. I casually asked about the sign and was told that the company was overhauling large diesel engines for the government of South Africa. I didn't pursue the matter, being predisposed to believe that the engines in question were tank engines.

Armed with this "information," I approached the editors of *Today Magazine* with a scandalous story. They were impressed, and I received a handsome advance to write an article.

However, once I began doing the serious research, some very disconcerting facts emerged. The engines were not tank engines after all—they were designed to power coal-hauling trucks! The Canadian government had issued export permits for this purpose, and nothing about the transaction was illegal. Meanwhile, my advance had gone into paying my rent.

The cost of my unverified assumption was the extra month of unpaid research I had to do in order to salvage my article. The story now focussed on how, with Ottawa's support, several Canadian companies were shipping "civilian arms"—components that could be used for both a military and civilian application—to repressive régimes.

This episode brings home an important lesson to the prospective researcher: Gathering random facts does not necessarily mean obtaining information. Information is obtained through a *process* by which facts are gathered, organized, compared, and balanced in a logical manner. In my unfortunate experience with the would-be exposé, I left out much of this process in the critical early stages.

This book shows you how to acquire information to meet your information needs quickly, cheaply, and efficiently. Much of the information you want is free for the asking or amazingly inexpensive.

The book is divided into two sections. Part One explores the process of gathering information. The first chapter summarizes the principles of research, and the following chapters contain edited interviews with specialists in different fields who reveal their favourite research techniques. For example, historian J. M. S. Careless explains how he researched his award-winning biography, *Brown of The Globe*. Police instructor Arthur Roberts discloses tricks that police use to gather information. An anonymous skip tracer shows how he finds missing persons by using a telephone and a few reference books. Well-known lawyer Julian Porter discusses how his old-fashioned, straightforward methods of research have helped him win some challenging cases. And John Zaritsky gives an inside view of investigative journalism.

Part Two of this book examines some of the key sources of information available in Canada: federal, provincial, and local government records, court documents, and library resources. The samples of these that are reproduced show what a remarkable range of facts can be accessed through local public offices.

Some of this source material will change in the coming years, but the methods of finding it, and the knowledge of what types of information are available and how they are stored, will not. They will always help you fill any information need. Understanding these methods of retrieving information is far more important than knowing where a specific piece of information is kept.

Computer buffs may be surprised that this book downplays computer information retrieval services. This lack of emphasis is because it is my personal belief that most information that you can obtain from a computer can be found quickly by doing manual searches—using indexes and a good library. Computer searches can be expensive and are therefore available only to a minority of people. This book gives approaches of gathering information that *all* Canadians can use—usually free of charge.

One final point: Students who have attended my courses and seminars on research techniques often ask if they should misrepresent themselves or even lie about who they are and why they want certain information. Journalists, too, have asked me this question, because some of their research involves sensitive topics. At times it's a tempting option, when you know you can obtain the material you want more quickly and easily by stretching the truth. But my response is that there are so many sources of information available in Canada to anyone that it hardly makes sense to create potential problems for yourself by lying. If one avenue closes to you, there are many more to choose from.

APPROACHES
Part One

The Principles of Research

Chapter One

There is no single method for gaining access to information. The processes, and appropriate sources, obviously vary from problem to problem, but there are certain principles that are common to all of them.

Begin by posing the question: "Why do I want this information?" This leads you to examine the context and kind of information to be gathered. For example, three different specialists asked to investigate family life among seventeenth-century Iroquois Indians would supply three different kinds of information. A sociologist would supply information about the social aspect of Indian life. A lawyer would no doubt give an account of the laws of the tribe. An historian might combine aspects of both kinds of information, along with other facts.

Acquiring an Overview

Your second question should be: "Am I ready to start my research?" Research is like reading: We bring meaning to the printed word, not the other way around. Having knowledge of a subject, we are able to understand what an author is trying to convey; otherwise, we could just open a textbook on advanced electronics and read. Most of us, however, need an *overview* of a topic in order to understand it. Without this overview, it is difficult to formulate specific research questions. Sometimes acquiring an overview can take longer than the actual research. You may have to read several books and interview many experts before coming to grips with a subject. But sometimes an appropriate book or article in an encyclopedia—even telephoning one expert—can suffice.

I was once asked to write an article for *Canadian Building* magazine on air rights in the construction industry. Because I didn't understand what air rights were, it was impossible to formulate specific questions in order to interview authorities on the subject. Magazine articles in my public library defined the concept: Air rights are rights to lease or buy space above buildings, including transactions known as density transfers. I learned that air rights had been part and parcel of city planning for centuries. For example, the City of London leased air rights in 1209 to shopkeepers along London Bridge, permitting them to build and extend their shops upward. In the 1920s the Illinois Central Railroad leased the air rights on its property to developers to encourage development along an Illinois river.

Without this overview I could not have formulated intelligent, specific questions about what was initially a confusing concept.

| Formulating and Refining Questions | Refining questions is an art in itself. Computer operators are very aware of this. A broad request to an experienced computer operator, |

such as: "List articles on the economy that appeared in Canadian newspapers in 1983," would never be acceptable. A badly worded question like this wastes time and money and doesn't isolate useful information. The question could be reworked to be: "List articles describing the effects of high technology on Quebec's economy from July to December, 1983." (The use of computer data banks is examined in more detail in Chapter 14, "Using Libraries in Canada.")

Refining questions is half the battle in any research. A friend once approached me with this question: "Do you know of any jobs?" He had asked the same question of friends and employment agencies, but was having no success. There were jobs available, but his problem was that he hadn't narrowed down his question so that he could search for them.

First I helped him formulate detailed questions. I asked him what his assets were. He had a graduate degree in education, had been a

Y.M.C.A. director responsible for designing and teaching courses for five years, a director of a non-profit educational institution for eight years, and he spoke fluent Italian. He had grown up in an Italian neighbourhood in Toronto and preferred to work with Italians in a non-profit organization. He found this type of setting more agreeable than a large corporate structure. The discussion clarified the main issues, so that the question now became: "How can I find employment as an instructor of adults in an Italian organization in Toronto?"

Now we were able to formulate other specific questions: "What Italian social service organizations exist in Toronto?" "Are there any associations that hire adult instructors?"

Once the questions were formulated, the investigation was relatively easy. A telephone call to City Hall enabled us to compile a list of all Italian social service agencies in Toronto. My friend determined which of these agencies provided educational programs, and he contacted them.

A quick look through the *Directory of Associations in Canada*, available in the public library, pinpointed the Ontario Society for Training and Development, an association that represents instructors of adults. It meets regularly and shares information on job openings.

As you might guess, my friend found the job he wanted. Such success is never guaranteed, of course, but proper research techniques enhance one's chances.

People setting out to research a subject often suffer "information paralysis"—an inability to define their information needs. I have encountered many students in a wide range of professions who have faced this problem. Here are a few of the most common types of questions before and after the students refined them:

"How can I find a person?" became "How can I locate Mrs. J. W. Jackson, who moved to Vancouver last year?"

"How much money did Brascan make in 1983?" became "What was the after-tax profit of Brascan's operations for the first quarter of 1983?"

"How do I start a trade union?" became "What legislation governs the formation of trade unions in British Columbia?"

"How can I find out if a bank will seize the car I am about to purchase because the present owner has used it as collateral for a loan he may have defaulted on?" became "Where can I get information on automobile liens in Ontario?"

"Where can I find out about housing prices?" became "Where can I find a list of housing prices for the city of Halifax?"

"Is there a cure for baldness?" became "Can male pattern baldness be cured?"

"Is there a link between diet and cancer?" became "Have any studies shown a correlation between breast cancer and diet in North America?"

Secondary versus Primary Information
The above questions—in fact, most questions—have already been answered. Somewhere, at some time, an expert has answered part or all of your question. This narrows your research to *secondary* sources of information, and in nearly all instances this information is available either in print or by telephoning the source. Your goal, then, is to locate indexes of published material and directories of experts and organizations. Most public libraries keep these reference sources, and they are discussed in Chapter 14.

My students' questions were answered mostly by using indexes, directories, and government experts. The relative was located by calling Directory Assistance in Vancouver. A telephone call to Brascan Ltd. revealed the company's earnings. A librarian at the British Columbia Ministry of Labour mailed a copy of the appropriate provincial labour legislation. Information on automobile liens in Ontario was obtained by a visit to the Personal Property Registration Branch of the Ontario Ministry of Consumer and Commercial Relations in Toronto. A cross-Canada survey of housing prices was located in several newspaper articles. Several studies on baldness, as well as on breast cancer and diet correlations, surfaced in a directory of medical abstracts.

Using the Telephone
The telephone is a researcher's most valuable tool. I can think of only a few instances where I could not obtain information over the telephone. During my first few days as a copy boy at the *Globe and Mail*, I witnessed a remarkable feat. The *Globe* kept a police-band radio in the newsroom to monitor potential sources, and late one night a bulletin thundered over it. A police shoot-out was taking place on

Toronto's Madison Avenue. With seven minutes to the paper's editorial deadline, it was impossible to send a reporter to the scene, but everyone realized that heads would roll if the newspaper was scooped by another daily.

The city editor grabbed the typewriter and began pounding out the information as it came over the radio. After a few minutes he ran into the newspaper's library, searched through the city directory, and wrote down the telephone numbers of addresses near the house where the shoot-out was happening. He then telephoned neighbours and asked for a description of events. He not only met the deadline but also produced a tightly written story that appeared on the newspaper's front page the following morning.

Evaluating
Sources

In addition to limiting the amount of information you search for, you should learn to critically evaluate material by comparing your information with that provided by different sources. Also, try to discover if a writer or interviewee has a bias. Slanted material is not necessarily unusable—it may be used in context—but you must be aware of the bias in order to make good use of it.

Using Referrals

A researcher would like nothing better than to be able to tap one omniscient source. Alas, this is but a dream. Research, as you have probably discovered, often involves following up a series of referrals. You gather a fact in one location, and this source leads you to another fact. And on it goes until a picture emerges.

The producer of CBC's "Marketplace" once hired me to interview homeowners who had found the controversial urea formaldehyde foam insulation in their homes. The idea originated from a letter received by a homeowner who was suing her real estate agent. She had been told when she had purchased her house that it wasn't insulated with the foam, but in fact it was. The producer wanted me to look into similar cases.

I began by telephoning lawyers involved in this case and asked for referrals. They knew of a few cases, and, by following up each of them, I was able to document 30 cases in a few days.

Research As a   A good researcher needs to be able to interact
Social Skill   with people. Research is unquestionably a
                     social skill; people who get along with others
find it easier to access information than those who are antagonistic.
The best approach is to put people at ease. To achieve this, be
relaxed, well mannered, and conciliatory. An example comes to
mind.

I once profiled Queen's Counsel Maxwell Bruce upon his appointment as head of Ontario's Residential Premises Rent Review Board.
Bruce was then a director of Crown Trust, a Toronto firm giving real
estate and mortgage loans. This meant that the new rent watchdog
was a landlord with a potential conflict of interest.

Bruce appeared to be a nervous person, so I tried to put him at
ease. I consciously raised topics for which he had a passion—he was
very involved in environmental affairs, so we talked at great length
about them. I didn't ask him directly about any conflict of interest,
because this might have terminated the interview. Instead of taking
an aggressive stance, I slipped in a seemingly innocent question,
asking him whether he planned to drop any of his other activities.
Bruce brought up the matter of Crown Trust himself and told me he
had resigned his directorship to avoid a potential conflict of interest.

I could sense I had put him at his ease, and we parted on friendly
terms. Later that evening he telephoned me at home to let me know
that he still owned shares in Crown Trust and that he in fact had not
yet resigned his directorship, but intended to shortly. I probably
wouldn't have learned this in any way other than by winning his
trust.

In the following chapters you'll read about other techniques used
by specialists in different fields. You won't need to master every
technique, but each one can be a valuable tool. For example, you are
unlikely to need to use interrogation techniques, but police instructor Roberts's procedures for background preparation may be helpful
in everyday interview situations. Use the edited interviews as a
guide to doing your own research rather than as a rigid formula.

Finding Missing People
Chapter Two

One of the toughest research problems is locating people who have changed jobs and addresses to avoid bill collectors. Professionals who find *skips*, as they are called in collection agency jargon, are known as *skip tracers*.

There is an art to locating missing people over the telephone. In this interview an experienced skip tracer, who has been a successful investigator for several large Canadian firms, shares some of his techniques.

This skip tracer, who wishes to remain anonymous, uses simple tools—city directories and telephone books. Most of the information comes directly from relatives and friends of the missing person. The challenge lies in persuading these people to divulge personal information without arousing their suspicions that a bill collector is in hot pursuit.

When I search for a person who has disappeared, I almost invariably attempt to reach their mother or another relative. I usually say that it's "Sam" calling and that I'm trying to reach her son. I say I have tried a telephone number, but it's no longer in service. When I read out the number to her, Mother usually tells me that her son hasn't lived there for a year. My response to that is: "Oh, I've been in Calgary for a year and just got back. I'm trying to look up my friends."

Today people are very suspicious of such calls. You practically have to tell Mother where her son's birthmark is before she becomes convinced that you are indeed a friend. She always wants to know how you know her son.

I can handle this question, because before an interview I have done my homework. I have already searched through old city directories to find her son's occupations over the years. I can tell Mother that I sat next to her son on the assembly line, that I used to put the clutch on, and he used to attach a wheel. This way I appear to be a friend.

Now I can ask Mother for a telephone number. I never ask for an address directly; if I did, she would become suspicious. Giving out a telephone number to a friend, however, is acceptable to her. Mother thinks that you can't find an address if you have a telephone number. But you can.

There are several ways to match an address to a telephone number. If you know a publicly listed telephone number, you can use a city directory. Telephone numbers are listed in these reference books in numerical order along with names and addresses.

A quicker method is to call the local telephone company. The company itself and police forces use special numbers to trace people. If you can get such a number, you can use the service, although it is not officially a public service. By giving the telephone number you've traced, you can get the exact address and correct spelling of a name, no questions asked.*

Finding an address for a privately listed number is trickier. Once again I call Mother, give her an old address for her son, and ask if he's still there. Sometimes she inadvertently tells me the street he now lives on, without stating the number. Then I call Directory Assistance and provide the correct name and street, along with a *wrong* street number:

"Do you have a listing for John Doe at 144 Avenue Road?"

The operator almost always corrects me. "No, I have a J. Doe at 154 Avenue Road, but it's an unpublished number."

Now I have the address. If I didn't have the unpublished number to begin with, I could easily get it now. I look up the street in a city directory and locate the man's neighbours. Neighbours generally give me a phone number if they believe I'm a friend.

---

*Author's note: In Toronto, for example, the number is (416) 977-2312.

As you can see, I often use city directories—not to be confused with telephone directories. A city directory enables you to look up a person by name, address, or telephone number. Some directories also list peoples' occupations. The directories are published annually by a variety of publishers across North America. Public libraries keep the most current copies for their local area. To look at back volumes, you generally have to visit the archives of the individual publisher.*

If I need access to an old city directory outside the city I work in, I call the local library or newspaper or university in that city and ask if they know of a freelance researcher. A freelancer can get the information for me quickly and cheaply.

Sometimes I cross-reference a listing with a telephone book to make sure the name is listed in the same way. Old telephone directories are easy to find. The first thing I do is find out the name of the local telephone company. In Ontario and Quebec, for instance, it is Bell Canada. Every Bell Canada directory from 1878 on is stored in the Canadian History Department of the Metropolitan Toronto Library at 789 Yonge Street. This reference library also keeps current and back copies of telephone books from other regions across Canada, although its collection is not as complete as that of the Bell Canada directories. It also pays to check with local libraries and provincial archives across Canada.

Here's another trick of the trade: I can contact the historical departments of the various telephone companies to get previous telephone numbers and addresses. For instance, I can call Bell Canada's Historical Department at (514) 870-7088 *collect* and learn the address and telephone number, from 1878 to the present, of anyone who ever had a telephone number listed in a Bell Canada directory. I need to provide a name, an approximate date, and the town or city the person lived in.

Let me give you an example of what I can do once I have a telephone number and address. I call the number during the day, expecting the person I'm looking for to be at work. His wife answers. I ask for "Joe."

Author's note: A useful booklet, *Catalogue of Directories Published and Areas Covered by Members of International Association of Cross Reference Directory Publishers*, lists many city directories and the addresses of the publishers. A free copy can be obtained from the association—refer to the Bibliography at the back of this book, under "Tracing People."

"Who's calling?" she asks.

"Sam, a friend," I respond.

This acknowledges that I know the man I'm looking for lives there. If I ask *whether* he lives there, she would realize who I was, and he would likely skip again.

Here is another way that this type of call might develop:

"Is Joe there?"

"No, I'm sorry. He'll be back at six."

"Is there any number where I can reach him?"

"Who's calling, please?"

"It's Sam, a friend."

"You can't reach him at work, because he works at a job where he can't be disturbed."

"Gee, that's funny. I thought maybe I could reach him there, just in case."

"No. Massey-Ferguson won't allow him to take calls."

I quickly write down that piece of information. I never ask anyone to repeat things, or else they might become suspicious. I pretend that I'm not the least bit interested.

Occasionally, someone will insist that I leave a number. I get around this request by saying, "Tell him Sam called. I'm back in town, and I'll give him a call around six-thirty, unless I have to leave again."

This line works. Normally my message is taken without any suspicion. When the missing husband returns home, his wife conveys my message, and he begins thinking aloud: "Sam...Sam... I must know someone named Sam. Who the heck is Sam?"

By making a simple telephone call like this, I often find out where the person works. And there isn't the slightest hint that a collection agency is arranging to garnishee his wages.

There have been cases where I have been given a telephone number and need to verify if a person lives at the corresponding address. In some cases I call and leave a message for the person to call "Sam," but the person refuses to return the call. This is when a letter can produce better results than the telephone. I write a letter to the person, care of his mother. I invent a subject—I don't state my real purpose in wanting to contact him. In the letter there is a confusing but interesting text that makes reference to page two. The catch is that there *is* no page two.

People are curious by nature. When they receive a letter like this, they find it hard not to write to me to point out that the second page wasn't enclosed. When that person writes me, there is a return address on the outside of the envelope—their home address.

Another letter I have used informs the missing person that a bank is holding a cheque in her name, and it will be sent to her if she completes and returns the attached form. The form is loaded with personal questions—from driver's licence number to date of birth. The letter explains that the information is necessary to verify that she is the right person.

The woman might be hiding from the police, but she will likely return my form, because she wants the cheque, which she figures is from an old account she's forgotten to clear.

There is nothing illegal about this approach, providing you *do* send a cheque. And I always do—for ten cents!

There are people who change jobs every six months and disappear, owing a lot of money. Sometimes their only relatives live in Europe. If this is the case, it's easier to locate them, because European families tend to keep in closer contact than North American families.

I can call a person's mother in Europe and get an address without paying a cent in telephone bills. Here is how I do it: I call the woman person-to-person, even though I know she lives in Canada. In fact, her mother tells me exactly that, through the operator. I then ask the operator if the mother has a telephone number for her daughter in Canada.

The operator might say, "No, she only has an address."

I would then say, "Operator, ask her what the address is so I can see if it's the same one that I have."

The mother normally co-operates with the operator and passes along an address.

I then tell the operator, "I've got that address, and she moved a long time ago."

Mother might reply, "I can't help that. I got a letter from her last month, and that's the only address I have."

The operator comes back to me. "I guess you lose."

Notice that I did not talk directly with the mother. I talked only with the operator, who acted as a middle person and helped me find an address that I know is only a month old. And because it was a person-to-person call, it didn't cost me a cent!

Operators are invaluable to me. If I know the person I'm looking for has relocated in another city and has an unlisted number, I call the operator. Here's an example:

"Do you have a listing for an S. Tyler at 123 Main Street?" I ask. (If the surname is a very common one, I make sure I have as many initials as possible to help narrow down the choices.)

The operator generally corrects me: "I've got a Tyler, S., on Timbuck Street. But I'm sorry, it's an unpublished number."

Now I know the street the person lives on. I use this piece of information and look up the street in the city directory for that city. I study the numbering system on the street. It is safe to assume that a person who moves frequently isn't going to live in a house alone. So I eliminate all the private houses, and I isolate rooming houses and apartments.

I call the operator again and ask for an S. Tyler, giving one of the possible addresses. The operator might say there's no listing for that person at that number, but there is an unlisted number *close* to that number. So I go back to the city directory, select a close number, and try the same thing again five minutes later. The idea is to keep asking an operator, using different addresses, until I have eliminated every possibility. Operators generally tell you if you have given a correct address, saying something like, "Yes, I have a person at that address, but it's an unlisted number."

Another trick of the trade is to contact a relative and leave a message, claiming I'm an old employer. I leave my private, unlisted number and my name, Sam, and ask to have the person call me *collect*. Meanwhile, I have learned from city directories what occupation he has. When he calls me, I can say I do the same sort of work, I've heard how good he is, and I want to offer him a job. That's only one of a thousand excuses I can invent. My only goal is the collect call, because my next telephone bill will list the number he has called from—that's likely his home number.

Tracing people involves a lot of psychology. Take a case where I have to verify that a person still has a particular car in his possession:

"Hello. Is this Wayne Jones?" is my opening question.

"Yes."

"Do you drive a '78 Ford?" I ask, knowing that he doesn't. I know what kind of vehicle he drives, because my collection agency is trying to get him to pay for it.

"Oh no, I don't. I drive an '83 Chevy Impala," he answers truthfully.

"Well, didn't you once live at 124 George Street?" I ask, once again knowing he didn't.

"No, I used to live at 124 Rox Street."

"Well, your licence plate is ABC 123."

"No, it isn't. Let me check...My licence plate number is DRC 159."

I write this down immediately and do not ask him to repeat anything—I get only one chance.

Every time he tells me something, it's the truth. He verifies that he is the person I'm looking for, that he still has the car we're after, and that it's still parked in his driveway. He has also verified beyond all doubt that he's the right man, because his last known address was 124 Rox Street. If I had *asked* him where he lived, he wouldn't have told me. If I had asked him what type of car he drove, he would have wanted to know why the heck *I* wanted to know—and he wouldn't have told me.

But by feeding him a lie, he instinctively tells me the truth to set the record straight and to convince me that I have the wrong person. He might ask me why I want the information. I tell him I sold my car to someone, and I'm trying to reach him.

Here is another case of psychology at work: I used to send letters to people who owed money but who had disappeared. I'd send the letter to them care of their mothers, stating that they owed $11,000 (when in fact they owed $1,000).

This would make people furious. They might not have called me if I had left the usual message with their mothers, but this way they were certain to get back to the S.O.B. who didn't know what he was talking about. Once I had the people on the phone, I'd start working them over!

Let me give you another example. I once tried to locate a paranoid writer—let's call him Charles Gagnon—because he hadn't made a payment on his car in five years. I managed to find a Charles Gagnon in Toronto, but I had to make sure it was the right one. I began by searching through city directories until I found another Gagnon, a Bob Gagnon in Calgary. I called Charles and asked for Bob.

Charles corrected me. "There isn't a Bob living here."

"You used to live on Heath Street in Calgary," I said matter-of-factly.

"No, I didn't. I used to live on Avenue Road in Toronto," he responded firmly.

I wrote this down. I had been suggesting that Charles was someone he wasn't, and he was proving that he wasn't the person by telling me something about himself.

Again I said, "You're thirty-five years old."

"No, I'm not. I'm forty-six."

Once I'd hung up, Charles may have sensed there was something odd about the call. He may even have checked with Directory Assistance in Calgary to see if there was a Bob Gagnon listed on Heath Street. Once he discovered another Gagnon, he would be certain I had the wrong person.

But the next day there was a bailiff in front of his house seizing the car he hadn't paid for!

Had Charles Gagnon's telephone number been difficult to find, I would have tried another approach. I would have asked myself: What does Charles do for a living? He's a writer. Most occupations are represented by unions or organizations, so I would have gone to the public library, used the *Directory of Associations in Canada*, and found the Periodical Writers Association of Canada, which represents freelance writers. The association wouldn't give me the number for Charles because he would have requested that it not be given out. But they would forward the message that Sam called.

Charles might not call me immediately. But when he couldn't figure out who Sam was, he'd become curious. So what would he do? He'd call Sam! Here is how this conversation would go:

"Is this Sam?"

"Yes."

"Do I know you?"

"Who is this, please?"

"Charles Gagnon."

"Charles. Gee, that name sounds familiar. When was the message left?"

"About a week ago. I can't remember when precisely."

"Oh, Charles! Didn't you once work at Cole's Bookstore?"

"No, no. I'm a writer."

"Now I know you. You used to live on Avenue Road."

"No, I lived on Fleet Street."

I'm in total control of the conversation. Charles is convincing me that I have the wrong guy, but, at the same time, he is inadvertently telling me personal information about himself.

People who go into hiding do not always assume a new street address. One case that taught me this involved a man who had taken out a $25,000 loan for a van and left the city without a forwarding address. I was able to locate his mother, but she would tell me only that she hadn't seen her son for five years. It was obvious to me from her tone of voice that she wasn't telling me the truth.

I tried a fresh approach with her. There is no one fixed approach, because dealing with people is not a science. I told her how I remembered her son buying a black van with lovely wide tires and how he had driven it to my home to show it to me. "It was a beautiful thing. How is it?" I asked.

She began to open up to me. "Oh, you know what he does now? He draws things on it!"

"Oh, what does he draw on it?"

I was gaining her interest when suddenly she began calling me Sam. Now we were buddies! She thought she remembered me from a party, when I was drunk. I don't drink, but I went along with this.

"I was embarrassed about that night," I said.

"Well, I won't tell you any more," she replied, trying to make me feel more at ease.

Having convinced her that I was a friend, she no longer hesitated to tell me what I wanted to know, nor did she pretend not to know where her son was. She told me he was living at a trailer camp nearby.

"What the heck is he doing there? Isn't it cold?" I asked.

"No, he's got a heater. He's working in the mine, and it's only a three-minute walk from where he's parked," she confided.

At this point all I knew was that he was in a trailer park near a mine—a vague description. But in a small town or rural area, the local city hall can be extremely helpful. In this case the town clerk informed me that there was only one trailer park in the area, and it was situated beside a mine.

I knew that the man I was looking for couldn't accept a telephone call during the working day, but this worked to my advantage. To verify he was in fact working at the mine, I called the company and asked to speak with him. The switchboard transferred me to the personnel department, and I was put on hold while they searched through their records. A woman returned and told me I couldn't speak with the man because he was working in the mine. This was my verification.

"I guess I'll have to call him at home. I have a number," I said, giving her a number that was close to what his number should have been. (I had looked through a local telephone book at a reference library and discovered that the first three digits for the town were always the same, so I used these three numbers and made up four others. In this way, when I presented the number, the woman believed it must be a local number. I sounded credible.)

She answered: "No, you're a few digits out. The number is such-and-such. But we're not allowed to give out addresses of employees."

Now I had the phone number, the name of the trailer park, the company the man worked for, and his company's verification that he worked there. Furthermore, the personnel department wouldn't dare tell him I called, because it's against company rules to release personal information about employees. My company was on its way to collecting the van!

Some skip tracers locate a person but then take an antagonistic approach, which makes the person relocate. You have to take a soft approach, or you put up a wall between you and the person. I remember an assignment I took over from a colleague in my company. I had only an answering service number with which to work, because the person had moved. I called this number and left my name.

When the man called me I proceeded in this manner:

"Gosh, how's everything going, Joe? How's the problem? I've been trying to find out what's wrong."

Joe answered, "What do you mean, what's wrong?"

I then identified myself and offered to help him sort out his financial problems. He explained to me that the other bill collector was an S.O.B.

"Well, you know, a lot of them are amateurs," I said. I consciously sympathized with him and blamed things on my fellow worker. "He *is* a real S.O.B.," I agreed.

Joe began to feel that I was more of a friend. He also felt I was practically the vice-president of the collection agency, which I was not.

"Look, if you don't like him, why not try so-and-so?" I suggested, passing along the name of another collection officer.

He agreed and even provided his new address. The only reason this worked was because I was sympathetic with the man. I knew he was angry, and when I calmed him down, he had a lot to say.

There isn't a best time to call people. I might wake up a relative at two o'clock in the morning.

"Where can I reach John?" I'll ask a father.

"I'm dead tired. Do you realize what time it is?" he might answer. Then he demands to know who's calling.

"This is Sam. Where can I reach Joe?"

"Don't you realize it's late at night?"

"Oh, I'm sorry. I didn't realize the time. I'm calling from Toronto. What's Joe's number?" I ask again.

Father will give me the number and say good night. The next morning he will wake up and ask himself, "Did I get a phone call last night?" He can't remember; he was in a semiconscious state. And no father wants to admit that he squealed on his son.

Sometimes I call a parent during the day and ask for their daughter, knowing very well that she hasn't lived at home for five years. I ask her mother, "Do you remember me? I used to live across the street at such-and-such an address." I will have used the city directory to locate where the mother lived five years ago, studied the numbering system on the street, and learned the neighbours' occupations at the time.

If the mother tells me her neighbours didn't have any children, I would immediately say, "Yes, they did. Don't you remember?" Usually she believes me. It's easier than calling me a liar, and, after all, she hasn't lived at the address for years—it could be true.

I'll proceed with other questions. "I haven't seen her for years. How's she making out now?"

"She's a writer now," says the mother proudly.

I often say, "How can I reach her? She'll be surprised to hear from me."

Most parents will give me the telephone number, because they think I'm one of the kids who used to play with their daughter. With that number I can now locate her.

One of my most difficult tracing assignments was to locate a man who had once owned an engine overhauling business with fifty employees. He had borrowed $1 million from a private financing company and then disappeared without a trace. No one knew it at the time. He was rarely in his office, and payday was only once a month. Finally, weeks after payday had gone by with no paycheques being issued, his employees became nervous. They visited his home and found it empty. They went to his bank and were horrified to learn that the account was empty—their boss had taken off with their money!

This was the only information that came to me, and it was already three years old. To find the boss, I began with his former address. I looked up his neighbours' telephone numbers, using old city directories. I called his neighbours at random and kept asking for leads on where he might have gone. One neighbour told me the man had always talked about moving to Prince Edward Island.

I then looked in an old telephone book to see exactly how he and his wife had listed their names. This is very important to do, especially when a common name is involved. An initial can make a big difference.

Once I located the proper listing, I called Directory Assistance for P.E.I. and gave the man's name in the same way it had been listed in the old telephone book. The operator told me that she had one listing at 12 Main Street. I listened carefully and wrote down the address. Usually operators won't give you an address if you ask for it directly, but they sometimes slip up. I was also given the publicly listed telephone number for this man.

I dialed the number and asked to speak with the man, using his first name.

A woman answered. "He's not here. I'm his wife, Betty. Can I take a message?"

"Yes, tell him Sam called. I won't be able to call him tonight, but I'll call him again tomorrow."

"Should I give him a number?" she suggested again.

"No. I'll be out, so I'll give him a call."

"Good. I'll give him the message," she replied.

This verified I had the right person, since my file indicated he had a wife named Betty. To make it nice, Betty was going to tell him that Sam called. He was going to rack his brains for a week wondering who Sam was. And before he could figure it out, the authorities would nail him!

A Journalist's
Notebook

Chapter Three

At only 27 years of age, reporter John Zaritsky won the first of many prestigious awards, the Ford Foundation Fellowship, to attend the Washington Journalism Center. There he was offered a job by the *Washington Post* as a cub reporter. Concerned that he would be spending his best years working on insignificant stories, Zaritsky turned down the offer, and the paper hired its second choice—Carl Bernstein.

Two years later, as an investigative and political reporter for the *Globe and Mail*, Zaritsky won a National Newspaper Award for a series of articles that revealed that Ontario cabinet minister Darcy McKeough had approved the subdivision of land in which he had a financial interest. Largely as a result of the articles, Ontario's conflict-of-interest legislation was tightened up.

Since 1975, Zaritsky has worked for the CBC as producer of its highly acclaimed investigative series, "fifth estate." Zaritsky's credits with "fifth estate" include some of its more contentious and controversial reports and an Oscar-winning documentary, "Just Another Missing Kid," an investigation into the death of 19-year-old Eric Wilson and the inefficiencies of the American judicial system.

Zaritsky explains that there is no mystery to research. For him it boils down to hard work and persistence. For him there are no hard and fast rules; rather, each story dictates a new approach to gathering information.

In this edited interview, he gives examples of when to use a "soft" or "hard" approach in interviews. He reveals how to win the trust of sources. In describing the McKeough affair, he demonstrates how to invent excuses that open the doors to information and where to go if these doors close.

Zaritsky also explains how he used basic sources for some of his biggest stories, including interviews with municipal planners, land registry files, and company records available through the government. He cautions researchers against relying on only one source and provides a list of questions to ask when dealing with any source. Body language, and the techniques he used to con a con into releasing RCMP documents, are also explored.

There is a philosophy that I adopt in all my work: I don't want *any* surprises. I want to learn everything there is to know about a particular subject—and from every conceivable angle. If I am working on an investigative story, I always try to put myself in the position of the person I'm interviewing; I try to anticipate what their defence may be. Otherwise, I may end up with a surprise that can devastate my story. In my work I have to be very complete.

Perhaps the biggest research challenge of my career came when I was at the *Globe and Mail*. I got a tip from a stranger who would not identify himself and was quite nervous and agitated on the telephone. He told me that when Darcy McKeough had been Ontario Minister of Municipal Affairs, he had approved the subdivision of some land that he owned or had a financial interest in. On the surface, it was a great story: It meant that McKeough had a direct conflict of interest, because he had used his public position for his private gain. But what the source didn't know, or was unwilling to say, was where the land was, nor would he say where he had acquired this information.

I began the research in the most logical spot—in Chatham, where McKeough was from. I went there to acquaint myself with the town and find out about the subdivisions that had been built around it.

I went to the town hall and created some very innocuous reason for my interest. You can get a lot of information out of people as long as you seemingly don't have any bad reason to want it. I said the *Globe* was doing a story on towns and cities and on the growth problems they were experiencing. I spent a week or two learning what the town limits were, what growth the town had experienced, and talking to a lot of town planners to determine the kind of subdivision of land that had occurred in the area.

It was a very difficult situation. This was Kent County, and the McKeough family was wealthy and established. Darcy McKeough was a local hero and was known locally as the "Duke of Kent." The least sign that I was trying to expose a highly prominent man—the local Member of Parliament and the second most powerful man in the Ontario government—and the doors would have closed immediately.

During these initial weeks of research, most of my information came from interviews. There was no way I could do the title searches without getting a lot of people nervous about what I was doing. After a few weeks I still didn't have the proof of what I had been told over the phone; I didn't know whether there was even a grain of truth to it. But by then I was familiar enough with Chatham to start my research in the local land registry office. I started searching the titles for a lot of the newer subdivisions. I didn't know what McKeough owned; I just kept searching and eventually found a number of companies that had sold land for subdivisions in the Chatham area. Then I simply copied the names of those companies, went to the Companies Services Branch of the Ministry of Consumer and Commercial Relations in Toronto, and researched their boards of directors. Lo and behold, McKeough's name appeared on one of the boards, and then his brother's name appeared.

Then the delicate task began—determining whether the minister himself had signed the documents approving the subdivision, or whether they had been signed in his name by a bureaucrat. To answer this question I started, in a general, unintimidating way, to learn how subdivision controls worked. I wasn't after specifics at this stage, just general information on the process. I drew up a list of questions: How was a subdivision approved? What was the involvement of the ministry? What did the minister do? What was his power? Did he ever reject an application?

I established that the minister had real power and wasn't a rubber stamp figure. Then, having established the general process, I moved on to the case in question. Once I knew how it was done for all subdivisions, I could finally ask: In this specific instance, was this process carried out?

The final answer was yes, it had. The minister had actually signed the documents. The series of articles on this subject led to McKeough's resignation.

Another important guideline I follow when researching a topic is: I try to avoid trusting one source. Always examine the motivation of people. Ask yourself: Why are they telling me this? What's in it for them? Who are they? What axe do they have to grind? Always be aware of the fact that people give you information for a reason, so check and recheck and confirm from other sources. A one-source story is a very dangerous story. But also keep this in mind: Even though people have an axe to grind, don't let it stop you from using their information. Sometimes the information can be accurate—and most important—provable.

Here is a case in point: I once worked on a story that involved a man who had broken into an RCMP detachment in Eastern Ontario. He had rifled the safe and stolen confidential documents. I was working for the *Globe and Mail* at the Ontario provincial gallery at the time, pursuing a number of investigative stories. I received a call from Morton Shulman, then a Member of Parliament. He had been contacted by this man, who was trying to sell him the stolen documents, which he said included evidence that the Mounties had been using juveniles as paid informers without their parents' knowledge or consent. Shulman said he couldn't touch the story, but he could put the man in contact with me.

The *Globe* and I then faced a real problem, because if we bought the documents, we could be charged with receiving stolen property. We certainly didn't want to pay for the information, but at the same time we wanted as much of it as we could acquire, because it sounded as if the public had a legitimate right to know about it.

I held a series of hair-raising meetings around the Ontario legislature with the man, but at some point the Ontario Provincial Police became aware of them. So the meetings had to become even more clandestine. I kept leading the man on, saying we weren't really sure he had anything that was worthwhile and that he would have to give us proof that he had what he said he had.

Finally he fell for it and produced a list of the RCMP informers and the amounts they were paid, their names, their ages, and everything else to prove that he had all this other material. The "other material" included documents on what to do in case of a nuclear attack, none of which I was keen to acquire. What I really wanted was what he gave me. We got our story.

My involvement with the "fifth estate" documentary, "Just Another Missing Kid," began when we were approached by the parents of the murdered youth, Eric Wilson. They knew part of the story, but only part. They saw things from their own perspective, as parents of a missing son. They explained their experiences with different police forces, their own search for Eric through Nebraska and Colorado, the lack of co-operation and the indifference of the authorities they had met. One of the things they couldn't understand was why the killer of their son had been arrested in Eric's van and subsequently released.

So our research addressed several questions: What were the circumstances of the arrest? What charges had been laid against the killer? When had he been released? Why had he been released?

The circumstances of each story dictate the approach and philosophy you use to gather information. In this case we went to the American police and judicial authorities, including the Assistant District Attorney who had been in charge of the case. And rather than adopting a tough, hard-nosed, adversarial stance, we approached them as Canadians who were unfamiliar with the American judicial system and, like the family, simply didn't understand how these rather strange and seemingly inexplicable events had occurred. We asked them to please help us, as foreigners, understand the situation. Brian Vallee, the associate producer working with me, and I talked to these officials briefly over the telephone at first, in a neutral fashion, then visited them and spoke with them extensively for several days. We told them that we wanted to understand the American judicial system as it worked in this particular case. This approach put them more at ease, especially because they were themselves quiet critics of the system. We wouldn't have won their support had we used a "Sixty Minutes," guns-drawn approach, demanding, "Why, Mister D.A., did you let this hoodlum go when you clearly had him?"

A lot of researchers approach their work with preconceived notions about what has actually happened, who the good guys and the bad guys are. Their know-it-all attitude is quickly picked up by their potential sources, who often sense this hostility and built-in bias. Instead, the researcher's or investigative reporter's primary purpose should be to encourage the subject to talk. This is a cardinal principle. Anything that accomplishes the goal of people relaxing and talking to you yields better results than if you do a lot of the talking to show you know what it's all about. In a sense it boils down to submerging your own ego. Sometimes you have to play dumb.

The biggest difference in my approach to research now as opposed to when I began 18 years ago is that I'm a lot softer. I play dumb more often, I'm far more neutral, and I concentrate more on listening than on asking questions. I approach people in a more open-ended way, and I am really willing to listen to everyone's side of the story; as a result, I think I get harder stories now.

Your approach also depends on the constraints of time and money. First, establish some sort of communication with the subject. Bear in mind that a lot of people are busy. You can't, for instance, interview a cabinet minister and fish around for neutral subjects to discuss. However, approaching a topic slowly is often the best policy, even by talking about something as mundane as the weather or the town you live in.

The best kind of interview is arranged on a person's home ground—at their house, as opposed to their office. Restaurants and bars aren't a great idea, because they are public places; some people are nervous about talking in public. Your object should be to win people's trust and confidence. You achieve this by proving you are a sympathetic and understanding individual who isn't going to expose them and that you are doing something worthwhile, something they can believe in.

I obtained police and court files through my contacts on the "Missing Kid" story by adhering to these principles. These records were, of course, invaluable, because my task was to find out everything about the lives of the two killers, from the time they were born until the time they committed the murder.

I also had to interview a lot of different people, some of whom were not always honest, so I used their body language to tip me off when they were about to lie. I can tell when people are fudging, because I look a lot at their eyes. Eye contact tells me a lot: Very few people who are about to lie look you right in the face—there is always some slight movement around the eyes that breaks eye contact. This goes back to our childhood. We rarely ever looked into our parents' faces and lied. It's ingrained. One man I interviewed for "Missing Kid," for example, lied and lied and lied. And at times he also told the truth. But when he lied, there was a nervous twitch on one side of his face; it was almost imperceptible, but it was reliable.

Here's another important rule for me in any story I'm working on: Never betray a source. It pays to stick to this rule. In the early 1970s, I wrote a series of articles for the *Globe and Mail* about the Ontario government's purchase of land from a company with several prominent Tories on its board of directors. The directors had bought the land cheaply and sold it shortly after to the government for a healthy profit. The articles led to an official inquiry in which I was a star witness. The entire focus of the inquiry became how I had acquired my information. The judge ordered me to divulge the names of my sources. I refused. He threatened to throw me in jail. I still refused. He finally decided not to make a martyr out of me and instead fined me $500. It was a great boon for me, because it established, publicly, that I would not betray a source. Thanks to the Ontario government, I was given impeccable advertising to enable me to carry on my work. From that point on, nervous civil servants remembered that I had stood the test.

As I mentioned earlier, the circumstances of each story dictate my approach. Sometimes it's extremely difficult to even confront the key person. Let me give you an example.

I worked on another series of articles for the *Globe* about certain firms who were receiving an inordinate amount of business from the Ontario government without submitting tenders. One company was owned by an individual who was well shielded from reporters by his secretaries. I could never get through this protective office shield. To talk to him, I first found out where he lived. I knew his name and used the Might Directories at the library to find his home address. I knew from chasing him around his office that he left work around five and that, given the length of the drive from his office to his home, he would arrive home at about five-thirty. So I made sure that I was at his home at five-fifteen. He clearly knew I wanted to speak with him, and he had been avoiding me. When he arrived, I simply got out of my car, gave him my name, said that I had been attempting to reach him for a number of days, and here I was. He didn't have anything to say to me, but he did say, "No comment." That was crucial information at that stage; until then my only information had been that he was unavailable for comment. This new information, one sentence in a story, revealed that he had had a chance to offer some explanation.

There are no hard and fast rules in research. Although I've pointed out that playing dumb in interviews can work, I must admit that I have had to be very hard-nosed on a number of occasions. I've interviewed people using a very tough approach and pretended that I knew a lot more than I actually did, in the hope that they would present their side of the story. I've worked with other reporters and used a classic police technique, "good cop, bad cop," in which one reporter plays at being on the interviewee's side and the other is hostile. You create conflict with the other reporter and try to force a confession out of the person you are interviewing. This technique has worked, too.

I took this approach with one of the best investigative reporters in the country, Gerald McAuliffe, on stories for the *Globe*. We were after Ontario civil servants who were trying to hide shady land deals, including purchases of land along the Niagara Escarpment. In one interview McAuliffe played the tough guy and became verbally violent and accusatory. I asked him to leave the room. Then, in the privacy of the civil servant's office, I explained that McAuliffe was a hot-headed individual who sometimes got carried away. It was difficult to put the brakes on him, so to protect himself, the government official should give me his side of the story. I told him I could understand he was being browbeaten and unfairly accused. I also said that if he would explain his side, I would do everything I could to make sure McAuliffe understood that there was indeed another point of view. The official then began to reveal a story far more implicating, and reaching a higher level of government, than we had imagined possible.

I have also found it advantageous to work on stories with another researcher. Each person operates as a brake on the other, so you don't get carried away. You have someone to help you recheck your facts and ensure that the story is accurate.

I have mentioned that you can get a lot of information out of people as long as you don't seem to have any bad reason for wanting it. I used this approach when I wrote the land story, referred to on page 26, which led to the Ontario government inquiry. The articles, roughly told, stated that the Ontario government had purchased 506 acres of land for a park at the forks of the Credit River, northwest of Toronto, from a corporation called Caledon Mountain Estates Limited. I found out that the company's board of directors included several prominent Tories. These board members had purchased the land for $805 an acre and resold it to the government within two years for $1,450 an acre. Had these Tories been tipped off through their political connections that the land was going to be used to create a park? Had they taken advantage of inside information?

I started my research by searching the land titles of the properties involved; they told me the original purchase price and the history of each piece of land in question. Then I had to establish that certain board members were highly placed Tories. This was tricky, but I concocted a quite innocent reason why I wanted a list of all the delegates who had attended the 1971 leadership convention that had resulted in the election of William Davis. The Conservative party gave me the list of all the delegates; I compared the names on this list with those of the land purchasers and found some of them to be the same.

After the first stories started to appear, one ministry began to refuse to give out information. There was a high degree of paranoia, and I soon realized that I wasn't going to get any information out of that ministry. So here's another principle in research: If you can't get the information from one source, try another. A lot of the same information is kept in several government departments, so you have to find the department that will give it to you.

In this instance, that's precisely what I did. First of all, I tried to understand how government, and in this case how the Ontario government, went about purchasing land. I found there was another department that handled the actual mechanics of land purchasing. With the heat of one specific department, and understanding how land purchasing occurs, I approached the other department. Again I used a seemingly innocuous reason for my inquiries. I located a middle-level civil servant who gave me the information that was absolutely confidential elsewhere: what the government had paid for the land. Until then that hadn't been made public.

When I joined CBC's "fifth estate," I used a lot of the same basic techniques I had employed as a print journalist. For instance, I once worked on a documentary on the Canadian International Development Agency (CIDA). I didn't want to produce a traditional documentary on foreign aid, discussing the terrible needs and poverty of the Third World, nor did I want to do another show on the screw-ups of CIDA. I saw much more fundamental problems with the Canadian foreign aid effort. In the end I found that under the guise of helping the needy, Canada was basically helping inefficient, non-competitive industries at home. It was allowing them to foist inappropriate technology, products, and services on the Third World—all in the name of charity and foreign aid. This really wasn't appropriate, nor was it helping the people whom Canadian citizens wanted to help.

That was an exhausting, six-month research effort conducted by myself and Mary Frances Morrison. We started the research by reading every piece of literature we could find on foreign aid. This gave us a rudimentary grasp of the subject, the facts.

Then we talked to as many experts in Canada as we could find. Some of these contacts emerged from the literature search; others were obtained by contacting universities. We had to find people locally, because our funds didn't permit us to travel outside Canada to do research. We had to know the situation before we left Canada to film the story. And the only way we could find out what had happened in countries thousands of miles away was to talk to people who had been there.

The Third World countries were not anxious to be critical of foreign aid programs—in a sense, to bite the hand that was feeding them. We were not allowed into Botswana, where there was a project we were particularly interested in and one we thought was a good case study for bad foreign aid. To get into the country, we disguised ourselves as tourists carrying Kodak cameras. Then we travelled to the "Sudbury of Botswana," an area where there was nothing but an awful iron smelter. We aroused the suspicions of the local secret police and had all sorts of wild adventures as a result.

The object of our visit to Botswana was to film the CIDA project. To do this we had to sneak a film crew into the country from South Africa. The crew had convinced the Botswana authorities that they were doing a wildlife film for the South African Broadcasting Corporation. It worked. We met the crew at the smelter, got our footage, and were able to show what CIDA money had built, as well as the squalid conditions the workers lived in.

I must caution prospective researchers about the stories I've described. It is true that there are stories, such as the one about the stolen Mountie records on page 24, for which you can obtain the information you need if you can talk to the right person and if you handle your source properly. But a lot of stories are not like that; a lot of stories do not involve one magical fount of knowledge that you can tap and then come away with the entire story. Many stories are like working on pieces of a jigsaw puzzle. You fit one piece in one place, and it enables you to fit in another piece somewhere else. Two pieces enable you to fit in the third piece, and so on.

Getting Tough
Chapter Four

Meet Arthur R. Roberts, a leading police instructor and an expert on forcing criminals to talk. He spent 35 years with the Calgary Police Department and retired as the commanding officer of its Detective Unit. Today he is Director of Security for Atco Limited, an international, Canadian-owned firm, and lectures on interviewing and interrogating techniques to police forces across Canada.

Most of us can avoid an interrogation to get information. Nevertheless, the preparation that Roberts recommends, and other observations in this edited interview, reveal principles that can be applied in everyday interview situations.

Interviewing is an art that can be learned, but it is not a science. It cannot be rigidly guided by a fixed set of rules or principles. It is your personality combined with the skills you have acquired that lead to success. The only way to become an efficient interviewer or interrogator is to gain experience through practice. Remember the words of Sigmund Freud: "Man loves to talk. He cannot keep a secret. Truth oozes out of every pore."

I believe this. People can't keep a secret—all you have to do is make it easy for them to talk. Eighty per cent of all people will confess to a crime; the trick is to make yourself easy to talk to. Give them an ear to listen to and a shoulder to cry on. Ask the right question in the right manner at the right time, and they will give you the right answer.

There are two basic techniques of obtaining information: interviewing and interrogating. An interrogation is an interview with stress. In an interview we ask questions without creating stress; in an interrogation we ask questions that create psychological stress.

Whether you interview or interrogate, you have to find the answers to six basic questions: who, what, when, where, why, and how. The answers to these questions form part of the interviewing or interrogating package.

You must be a good listener, and you must listen with your ears, your eyes, and your heart. The fact that you are sitting quietly and listening does not necessarily mean that you understand what the subject has said. You have to listen in a two-dimensional manner. First, listen to the main point rather than the periphery. Many people become too interested in small details and do not pick up the main point of what is being said.

Second, evaluate what is being said by studying the subject's behaviour and manner of expression, the sound of his or her voice, and anything else connected with the subject's appearance. You should listen empathetically to understand the person and evaluate the testimony.

You are more likely to get a person to talk if you can develop a rapport. Before the interview, greet the person cordially, show respect, and find some common bond or interest. Don't necessarily start your interview with the main questions, but rather put the person at ease by talking about something you both share an interest in.

When interviewing, let the person tell his or her story—*uninterrupted*. Don't ask sudden questions. At the same time, do not allow any "dead points" in the conversation, or you will lose control. Don't ask questions that require only yes or no answers; otherwise, you end up doing most of the talking. Also, don't ask leading questions—they influence the answers you get.

Your last question should be something like: "What else do you think you can tell me?" or: "Is there anything I have not asked you that you thought I was going to ask you?" or: "Can you think of anything else?"

I find that a successful interview contains six elements, which I remember by making a mental checklist using the letters of the word *polite*:

• Planning and preparation: Learn everything you can about the case beforehand, and jot down key questions.

- Opening remarks: Decide what it is you are going to say in the beginning, introduce yourself, and describe your credentials. Explain the purpose of the interview. Look for common interests, then develop a rapport.
- Listening: Do not interrupt the subject. Learn to listen, but maintain eye contact and take your time.
- Interviewing: Keep your objective in mind. Obtain accurate information. Maintain control of the interview. Remember to ask who, what, when, where, why, and how.
- Thinking: Look for symptoms of deceit in the person's behaviour. Have you asked the key question? Have your objectives been met?
- Ending: End the interview in a courteous, friendly manner. Shake hands with, and thank, the person. Summarize the interview for him or her. Make it easy for the subject to pass along other information to you by leaving your name and telephone number. Try to leave your subjects happy; if they like you, they'll call again.

In an interrogation, you take of course a completely different approach. The very word indicates a difference: It conjures up visions of baseball bats, assault, and various forms of torture used in order to force the person to confess.

Nothing could be further from the truth. The efficient interrogator has no need for violence and probably uses subtle, *psychological* pressures to pave the way for the person to confess to a crime.

Interrogating involves preparation—lots of it. Performing artists prepare themselves for their audiences; likewise, you must fine-tune your interrogation to suit the subject. Attempt to gain knowledge of the crime, the suspect, and your own abilities as an interrogator. Also, it's useful to prepare a "personality profile" of the person to help you phrase your questions. Here are some questions to ask yourself when preparing this profile:

- Who is your suspect? Make sure the full name is spelled correctly and that you can pronounce it properly, or else the suspect will think you know very little about him or her.
- What is the person's address? This may give you an indication of his or her socio-economic status.
- What is the person's age? A 25-year-old interrogator may find it difficult to attack a 50-year-old suspect by claiming greater experience.

- What is the person's occupation? This gives you an indication of how to talk to the suspect. You must be flexible enough to talk to a minister one minute and an illiterate ditchdigger the next.
- What is the suspect's work reputation? It can be helpful in inflating or deflating his or her ego during the interrogation. Using police liaison or public court records, attempt to find out if your suspect has a criminal record.
- What is the person's rank in the family? Try to find out if the person is the oldest or youngest sibling, and remember your own childhood experiences and where you stood in the family "pecking order."
- What is the person's ethnic background? The person may never look you in the eye because this is considered a sign of rudeness in his or her culture, so don't interpret it as a sign that the person is lying.
- What is the person's marital status? Is the spouse the dominant partner? Can you use the children to obtain a confession?
- What is the person's educational background? This gives you information about his or her inclinations and way of thinking. There is a difference, for instance, between the way a student of law and a student of drama look at the world.

Never tell your subjects that you do not know what is going on or that their information is false. If you do, you destroy the reliability of the interrogation process.

To interrogate is to act. You must be flexible and have a variety of techniques to draw upon to obtain a confession. You must have a high level of perseverance and a low level of frustration; you must be able to laugh or cry at a moment's notice; you may have to appear religious or seem to know every dirty trick in the book.

Appearances are also important. Because we want to build relationships of authority and subordination during the interrogation, the interrogator must appear as an authoritative person. Do not enter the interrogation room wearing a T-shirt, blue jeans, and Adidas. A slightly conservative appearance can help a lot to create an impression of authority.

The setting for the interrogation should be carefully planned. The main factor that helps a suspect confess is privacy. There is an inner pressure to confide in someone, but usually in one person at a time and in a private setting. So your interrogation room must be isolated from interruptions of any kind, including phone calls.

Sit close to the person. This can create a great deal of anxiety, which is what you want. Try to speak the subject's language to prevent misunderstandings between you. But don't lessen your authority by using obscene or insulting expressions; authority requires self-respect and mutual respect.

The physical conditions of an interrogation room vary, of course, but ideally, sit at a small desk in a small, windowless room. The desk should be in the corner of the room, and the subject's chair should be at a 90-degree angle to yours. The subject should sit with his or her back to the door. This type of set-up reduces distractions and creates intimacy and pressure.

Avoid a cluttered desk. Several files might encourage the suspect to waste time in the hope that you will go on to another case. One file can create the impression that the interrogator has lots of time to get the information.

Your desk should be clear of anything that might release the subject's tension. For example, removing ashtrays creates anxiety for the smoker. However, if the suspect has recently quit smoking, you may find that if you light up a cigarette the smoke may irritate his or her throat. Either way, tension is created that may lead to a quicker confession.

During the interrogation, always study body language. Look at the person's eyes: Are they shining or dimmed? Look at the mouth: Is it scowling or nervous? Follow the movement of the eyes and what direction they face. Look at the hands and legs: Does the suspect clench and unclench his or her fists? Does the person search for a place to put his or her hands? Does the person stand easily? Or does he or she shift the position of the legs every so often? The answers to these questions tell you how much tension the suspect is feeling.

Body language is always more noticeable when you grill the suspect with tough questions. For example, if a crime was committed at one a.m., and you ask firmly, "Where were you at one a.m.?" the person may show signs of being nervous, whether or not he or she is innocent. But if the person is guilty, the question should reveal various kinds of the body language I have mentioned—beyond mere nervousness.

A Private Eye Tackles Information

Chapter Five

In the world of private detective agencies, Intertel ranks near the top. It was established 15 years ago by some of the foremost intelligence people in the United States. Intertel's board of directors now includes the former heads of the National Security Agency, Scotland Yard, and the Royal Canadian Mounted Police.

The Canadian branch of Intertel was opened in 1971 by Calvin Hill, a former intelligence officer with the RCMP. Hill met the founders of Intertel while he was working in the U.S., on special loan from the Canadian government, to uncover organized crime. Intertel's directors were impressed with Hill, who had been with the RCMP for 22 years and had experience in many facets of criminal detective work, including planting bugging devices.

Surprisingly, Intertel acquires a lot of its information from public sources. And, as this interview with Hill reveals, a lot of information is acquired by using common sense approaches.

If we're hired to uncover how information has leaked from a company, we begin by drawing up a list of everyone who had access to that information. We find out where the topic was formally discussed and who was present at the time. Because of my expertise with bugging devices, I may "sweep" the room with special equipment to detect any electronic devices that may have been planted. The occasional bug has been planted to gain access to company secrets, but this method is highly overrated. There's not nearly as much of it going on as you read about. What we do as a rule is simply interview everyone who had access to the information, and we often uncover a lot of employee indiscretion. This is especially true in high-tech companies where employees know specialists in other companies. The employees divulge confidential information—not intentionally, but to impress their friends.

But that's only one type of problem we're called in to solve. Here's a different sort of case: A company once hired us because they suspected an employee had been harassing another worker. A woman had been promoted over a male co-worker, and shortly afterward, strange things began to happen to her. She received obscene telephone calls, and her office dictionaries were ripped apart. The male colleague was suspected, but there wasn't any proof.

Our first move was to interview six employees who had good records and weren't suspects. We interviewed these workers, because we didn't want anyone to know whom we suspected. We knew that once the interviews were over, they would talk to other employees. The workers didn't realize that we asked each of them a different set of questions, but we suspected that they would get together and come up with some common answers.

Then we brought in our suspect. He was shown into a large office and asked to sit in a particular chair that didn't have arms and was firmly planted so he couldn't move around. I sat at my desk about 15 feet away, my hands folded comfortably in front of me. This arrangement unnerved him before any questions were asked.

My partner sat at another end of the room, and we began firing questions at the suspect from two directions, making him feel the pressure even more. I would ask one question, and before he finished answering, my partner would ask another. We had the man going back and forth like a yo-yo.

We deliberately discussed the good management of the firm and talked about its clever president. Because our suspect had been overlooked in the company and felt frustrated, we suspected that this type of discussion would disturb him. We kept on in this vein for about 20 minutes. Finally he blew up—he just couldn't restrain himself. Soon he told us about ripping up the dictionaries and then confessed to other things.

There are "softer" approaches to gathering information. It used to be that if there was a problem in a factory, we would plant an undercover agent to report to management, but that practice caused problems. We no longer use this approach, partly because of changing labour laws. If you're going to fire someone, you have to give him or her just cause, so you would have to disclose that you had planted an undercover person among the employees. That would trigger morale problems, and any new employee would be suspected of being an agent.

Our present method involves doing what we call "attitude surveys." We find they're far more productive than the undercover approach and not as expensive. First, we announce on the general bulletin board that our firm has been brought in to examine the company. This notice asks for the co-operation of the workers.

Ninety percent of people are honest, but we have to give the company employee an "out" because of what we call the "rat-fink syndrome." Nobody wants to be thought a squealer. People may know what's going on in a company and disagree with it, and they may not be involved. But they don't want to disclose any information and therefore become involved. So we try to question people in such a way that we get the information we need without making them feel like informers.

For example, we've been hired to assess working conditions and morale inside a plant. We start by selecting the most junior person, say someone who has worked there for six months as a labourer. We ask him: "What would be the first thing you would do if you became the president of this firm?"

He may talk for an hour explaining what he would change and telling you the things he sees going on in the plant all day. Perhaps he doesn't agree with many of them, but he is pleased to talk, because nobody has ever encouraged him to express his feelings before. And because we're outsiders, not the boss, he can open up.

If you select 15 people from a staff of 100, you get a good insight into how that company is being run. In this cross-section will be several "retreads"—people who went to competing companies, then returned. These people are more likely to tell you what the sources of their problems have been.

We don't have rigid guidelines for solving each case, but we usually start with a track sheet identifying the problem and the appropriate investigative sources. Sometimes a company hires us to investigate internal theft—an employee may be running a similar business after hours, on the side, and stealing company materials and tools. In addition to checking on the suspect's lifestyle to see if it's compatible with her salary, there are several sources we use.

We consult the Companies Services Branch of the Ontario Ministry of Consumer and Commercial Relations, which tells us if a company is registered, its address, the composition of its board of directors, and in some cases if it's taken out a loan. Dun and Bradstreet records and local credit bureaus may yield personal financial information about the suspect. Newspaper clippings are an often overlooked source—they can be helpful for persons in the public eye. Court records can contain a wide range of information, including medical records and divorce settlements. Provincial land registry offices indicate land ownership. Voters' lists, available at any city hall, and city directories reveal a home address.

These sources can all be helpful. But quite often our information comes from interviewing neighbours. There is no set way to do this, but we normally knock on their doors and explain that we're inquiring about a person's financial situation. We approach neighbours in an informal way, and normally they co-operate, unless of course our suspect is in trouble with the law.

As you can see, there's no magic in uncovering information. There's no "Big Brother" handing us a file; it's really a matter of common sense. There is no one set way in which we operate. Instead, our approach is tailored to the particular problem. Here's a case we solved using an unorthodox method:

A company once asked us to investigate one of their vice-presidents. We read through the executive's personnel file and noted he had an advanced degree from a particular university. We suspected this wasn't true.

To verify the information, we contacted the university but, as is often the case with educational institutions, it wouldn't tell us anything. Without any verification from the university we couldn't tell our client that the degree was fabricated; if the employee was fired and in fact had a degree, he could sue the firm for wrongful dismissal. We advised the company of our suspicions and suggested that their personnel department send a memo to all the executives stating that the department was updating their files and required copies of any diplomas. Everyone co-operated except the vice-president in question. He complained but finally admitted that he didn't hold the degree after all.

Looking Back:
Historical Research

Chapter Six

During an introductory course on Canadian history, 800 students cram into a University of Toronto classroom that seats only 200. The lecturer they are waiting to hear is the eminent historian J. M. S. Careless, whose numerous texts are required reading in high schools across Canada. Among the books he has authored is a massive, two-volume biography of one of the founders of Confederation, George Brown. *Brown of The Globe* won the Governor General's Award for non-fiction in 1962.

In this conversation, Professor Careless explains how persistence paid off in acquiring the material for researching this biography. He also shares his approach to researching his latest project, an ambitious urban history of Canadian cities. Professor Careless believes a researcher must start his or her work by gaining a general knowledge of a subject and then refine specific questions. He stresses critically evaluating sources for their importance and shows how to accomplish this.

I started my research for *Brown of The Globe* while I was doing my doctoral thesis at Harvard University. The thesis was actually a study called "Mid-Victorian Liberalism in a Colonial Environment" and was not a biography of George Brown. It really only captured his views as seen through the *Globe*. Rather than publish my thesis, I decided to expand it into a biography, but there was a problem of finding sources.

Very little had been written on Brown except the occasional book. The key for me was gaining access to the personal papers kept in the Brown family. Another Canadian historian, Frank Underhill, had tried to do this before me, in the 1930s. He had approached the only living son of Brown, George Mackenzie Brown, who was living in Scotland. Underhill had received very courteous letters, but the answer was always the same: The papers were personal family correspondence. Furthermore, George Mackenzie was considering writing a biography himself. I wrote to George Mackenzie myself during the Second World War and received the same reply.

Then, when I was giving a talk to a local historical society, I ran into Brown's grand-niece, Catherine Ball. She told me she had seen the papers in the family home in Scotland, and the material looked interesting. She encouraged me to approach the family again, because George Mackenzie had died and because she felt that his children wouldn't feel the same way about the material as their father had.

Such a change in attitude seems to be a common thing. A father is often viewed as a personal figure, almost sacrosanct, as in this case. But George Mackenzie's sons, who were then in their late fifties and sixties, didn't have these feelings about their grandfather. They had heard he was a noble character and thought it was great that someone should write his life story, but they didn't think there was anything of any significance in the papers.

I took a chance on the value of the material, received a grant, and went to Scotland. I found a trunk full of personal papers and a lot of political letters to Brown; other family members had said they didn't exist, but they were just at the bottom of the trunk. The personal letters were mostly written by Brown to his wife, and there was absolutely nothing you would not have wanted to show to anyone then or now, because they contained his views of what was going on. His wife was a well-informed woman, and he was keeping her posted. I found letters that contained references to such things as John A. Macdonald coming into a cabinet meeting drunk again. It was very good material in every way. And it was much more than local colour—it was an inside view of Confederation by a man who was a major figure in it.

As is often the case, once I had this basic source, it led to other sources. I found nothing of the same significance, but other material turned up because I had this lead, sometimes just by pure serendipity. For instance, material from the estate of the former Liberal Prime Minister Alexander Mackenzie was suddenly turned over to Queen's University; it included correspondence between Brown and Mackenzie. This is the kind of development one learns of through the grapevine.

Sometimes it pays to advertise in newspapers and request information if you are researching someone who isn't well known. But everyone in the academic and historical community knew of Brown. I didn't need to advertise to trace his descendents, either, because an older family member had made the family history her life's hobby. She had stayed with the family in Scotland and painstakingly copied the birth and death entries from the parish register. She had even traced where the family members had moved. So I wrote to these people, who were all still alive, and in some cases learned useful information about the family. This information must always be recognized as questionable, but if an individual is remembered by various people in the same way, it's probably true.

To organize my findings, I used five-by-eight-inch file cards. Each card was an item in itself, and I used both front and back if needed. The cards were colour-coded under different headings. In fact, when I was working on the book, I assembled a large suitcase full of cards. If the ship taking me home from Scotland had gone down, I would have jumped overboard with my suitcase, and to heck with everything else!

Right now I'm working on a major book that examines the external relations of Canadian cities. I cannot go into their internal affairs as well, except insofar as they influence external developments. No one has tried to synthesize the whole historical pattern of urban-regional development on a large scale, but I think it plays a large part in giving us the kind of Canada we now have. I'm calling the study "Metropolis and Frontier." It actually focusses on the nineteenth century, because I think that was our major era of frontier building.

I started the research for this book by reading the material already in print, although not everything in one fell swoop—there was far more than I needed. I had already been reading material on cities over the years, so a lot of the work was already done. This doesn't mean I didn't need to go back and reread what I thought I had remembered from this book or that, because I didn't necessarily have notes on the information. I didn't bother to make notes on the general books if I just wanted to refresh my memory on a topic I knew something about. I also gathered very good material from theses and students' research papers.

Then it was time to move to the primary research. There are a number of major depositories of material on Toronto; for example, the civic archives (at the City Hall) keep city council records and reports from various departments. This is true virtually all across the country.

The major libraries throughout Canada are also valuable resource centres. They usually have made some attempt to gather material on their own town. Here you can also find diaries and business records of local private individuals. Another useful source are provincial archives, the holdings of which usually predate those of civic archives. Provincial archives also often store family papers.

In addition to these sources, there is the Public Archives of Canada in Ottawa. You can find masses of material there for filling in gaps. For instance, Board of Trade papers might be incomplete in one city, but you may pick up missing volumes in the Public Archives. There are also many private papers there on cities.

If you want to go beyond that in dealing with the internal history of a city, labour records are helpful. For instance, in Toronto I used material from the Typographical Union.

What you must do in research, in any case, is work from the general to the particular. That involves first orientating yourself. The mistake a lot of beginners make is to approach their subject too specifically, by looking up a published item on a particular place in a particular district, for example. They go immediately to the wider and primary data; maybe they get beyond it, or maybe they don't. Perhaps they want to research the life of a person; again they go to a library and ask: "What have you got specifically on that individual?"

Very often a helpful librarian can take you a long way on such questions. But more often beginners simply search out the articles or books by the titles and don't know enough about the subject to ask themselves what the critical inquiries are that need pursuing. Try to orient yourself about your subject *before* you go after the specific questions. This means, in historians' terms, scanning and comprehending the secondary sources available. Find what is useful in print. Once you already know something about the topic, you have a kind of grid in your mind that lets you say, "Well, I can screen this out, and I don't really need that. This is too general, or that's not the part that I want to cover."

Even an historian who supposedly knows a good deal about an historical event or person almost automatically starts by reading biographies (or even newspaper accounts) before zeroing in on the particulars. I repeat: Don't go to your primary, specific material until you cover the general.

In research, you have to establish a mental pattern of critical evaluation. I don't mean that you set up a neat, one-to-ten scale. But in your mind you start thinking that way. It is both common sense and also simply inevitable, once you begin to know something about the subject. You don't just say: "This is more significant than that." You are really asking: "How valid does this seem to me in forwarding my inquiry?" It's fair to add that you can't do much better than express this as "*seem* to me." One can proclaim a great deal about being objective and above bias, and it *is* important to try. But what you're finally saying is: "In my opinion (or in my now-informed judgment) this is the way I would rate this authority's material." The more you know about the subject, the more convincingly you can do it.

There are some common rules for this process of evaluation. For instance, the closer to an event the source record was made, the more likely it is to be valid. People are more likely to remember accurately what happened during or soon after an event than they are reminiscing about it 50 years later.

On the other hand, one must also take into consideration that when a source describes an event immediately or soon after, it may not have very much perspective on it. It may even be wrong about what happened. Consider our newspapers. They report that so-and-so got his head bashed in by so-and-so at four a.m.; well, it may be so, and it may not. They might print two days later: "Sorry, folks; it was three-thirty, and it wasn't him at all, and it was two other guys who did it."

This is human and natural, but it shows that against the immediacy of the source, you have to appraise the quality of information the source is likely to have. One way to judge this is by cross-testing: Compare one source against another, if you're lucky enough to have a variety. Then you can form your best judgment. It won't be the perfect judgment, but it will be the best one you can make on the basis of your most complete information.

A Cabinet Minister's Approach

Chapter Seven

Frank Drea's researching talents began to surface when he was an undergraduate student, and he graduated from Buffalo's Canisius College cum laude. With his high scholastic aptitude, he seemed destined to become a university professor. Instead, he became a journalist and eventually an Ontario cabinet minister (although he still manages to lecture occasionally at universities).

Drea was once an investigative labour reporter for the now-defunct *Toronto Telegram*, and it was there that he gained notoriety as an astute and relentless reporter with a penchant for uncovering corruption. His work was so widely recognized that the Canadian Broadcasting Corporation created a half-hour dramatic television series, "McQueen," based on Drea's life.

At the *Telegram* Drea created North America's first "Action Line" newspaper column, investigating consumer complaints. It was the prototype for many others.

He also wrote a series of front-page articles about five Italian labourers who were killed in a tunnel collapse on a sewer construction project in North Toronto in 1960. The articles were brilliantly researched and revealed several underlying issues: Italian labourers were being brutally exploited, safety regulations were being ignored, and the construction companies were getting kickbacks and evading income tax. The series resulted in a Royal Commission, the findings of which led to the tightening up of industrial safety legislation in Ontario, a more rigid system of inspections, the formation of trade union locals, and new minimum-wage laws. Drea was awarded the prestigious Heywood Broun Award for the articles—the first time a Canadian had ever won the honour. This is an American award usually bestowed upon such publications as the *New York Times*.

Now in his third Ontario cabinet post as Minister of Community and Social Services, Drea still does most of his own research. In this candid interview, he reflects on how he researched the tunnel disaster. Most of his information came from speaking directly with the workers and from carefully reading the legislation involved.

Drea, a former Minister of Consumer and Commercial Relations, also explores a few ways to gather information on companies.

There is always a reason *why* things are done. Once you understand the "why," you can make some sense out of them. You don't have to be an industrial engineer to investigate an industrial accident, but you can't investigate anything unless you understand some of the background. The real key to researching the Hogg's Hollow tunnel story was to talk to the workers themselves.

Briefly stated, the initial story was about how a private company had been contracted by Metro Toronto to install a tunnel under a section of the Don River. The company encountered quicksand and other impediments that hadn't been expected in the area. As a result, it decided to use much higher air pressure than usual to keep these impediments out while the labourers worked below. The tragedy began when a few of the men began to smoke. That caused a fire, which burned the insulation off the air hoses; the smoke overcame most of them. To worsen the situation, someone above turned off the air pressure, thinking that this would kill the fire and smoke. But the moment this was done the Don River came crashing in, along with tons of sand and dirt. Five of the six men were killed instantly.

The original story came to my attention when another labourer on the project walked into the *Telegram* office, asking to see a reporter. He had quit his job because of what he said were unsafe working conditions. So I had his allegation to start with.

The first thing to understand when beginning this type of research is that someone is in charge of the work site. So I asked myself: "What did this person (or persons) do or not do that allowed this to happen?" An accident like this occurs very rarely, so I also asked myself: "Was everything that was designed to prevent this kind of thing from happening functioning properly? Were there any safety regulations that applied in this situation, and were they followed?" In other words, I looked at the case the way a police officer would: There were five deaths in an industrial accident; I wanted to know what caused the accident.

At that time, Ontario had great legislation covering trench work, but no one ever enforced it. ("Trench work" means installing sanitary and storm sewers.) The unwritten agreement was that the government didn't have to enforce it, because the union's business agent would do it. But when this type of work was done outside of downtown Toronto, the unions weren't involved. It was the newly landed Italian immigrants who worked the suburbs; they couldn't work downtown, because they couldn't pass the screening exams, which were all in English. And as I learned from talking with these labourers, *anything* went on in the suburban areas.

I spent a little time gathering existing public records. Because this was a construction project, a building permit had had to be filed with the provincial government. This was public information. I wanted to see this permit, because I wanted to know who had approved the building plans. The permit told me that the Department of Labour, as it was then called, had done so on the basis of a submission filed by a person who claimed he was an engineer.

I checked out the engineer's credentials by calling the Association of Professional Engineers. It turned out that the man wasn't a registered engineer after all. That information opened up other avenues for me.

I also carefully read the department's Tunnel Regulations, which regulated underground work using compressed air. After interviewing various union officials, I learned that there was a printing error in the law. The word "minimum" had been used instead of "maximum"—if the labourers had followed the regulations to the letter, *every* worker would have died.

As is the case with any construction project, inspection reports had had to be filed with the Department of Labour. By reading these public documents, I found out that a government inspector had gone to the site but hadn't actually *inspected* the work being done. The report simply said he had *visited* the site, not inspected it. I probed a little further to find out why this was so. It turned out that there was only one department inspector for this type of work. He was about to retire, and because he had a heart condition, his doctor had forbidden him to go anywhere where there was air pressure. Everyone in the department knew this; it was no secret.

By this point my research, which was far from over, had revealed that this was a real "bucketshop" operation—really "Mickey Mouse."

The one worker who had escaped the disaster was a middle-aged Polish man who had survived cave-ins in Europe as a prisoner of the Second World War. He knew how to get out. But after this last close call, he went on a drinking binge for a week. No one knew where he was. A fellow employee gave me his address, and I waited outside his house for three nights in a row, from midnight until five in the morning. He eventually showed up, of course, and spoke with me, confirming the original allegation that the working conditions were far from safe on this job.

If I were researching this story today, some of the information would be easier to retrieve. I could get the building plans instantly from the Building Department at Toronto City Hall. The inspection reports mentioned earlier would be posted on the job site and filed with what is now the provincial Ministry of Labour. And using a word processor at the Workers' Compensation Board, I could quickly get a printout of the occupational health and safety record of any company. Even probing legislation would be easier today. You can visit the Ontario Government Bookstore on Bay Street and quickly purchase a copy of any legislation. When I was working on this story, I had to line up for hours on York Street.

While doing the research on the tunnel tragedy, other interesting information came my way. The workers told me that, on average, one Italian labourer was killed each month while working in the trenches in the suburbs. The provincial safety regulations required lumber to be used as bracing for this work and protective helmets to be worn. But this equipment was not used, because it was an additional expense for the employers. This was a clear contravention of the safety regulations. To follow up these allegations, I attended several inquests into the deaths of trench workers. I discovered a pattern: At the inquests, the fire department would say there was no lumber present when they dug up the dead worker. But a lawyer would always produce photographs of lumber sticking out of the ground; the lawyer would swear that there was so much lumber, they would have to burn it.

This was nothing less than a cover-up. Clearly, no one was enforcing the safety requirements, at least not in the suburban areas.

My research was beginning to paint an ugly picture. It showed that there were actually two worlds in Ontario: one for people who were born in this country, the other for Italian immigrants.

I learned of these atrocities by interviewing the people other reporters wouldn't talk to. There were 10,000 Italian labourers in the Toronto area then; most of them were newly arrived from Italy and didn't speak very good English. Ironically, they came from an advanced society in terms of industrial safety, while here in Canada they were being ruthlessly exploited. Contractors went so far as to hold back 10 to 20 per cent of their wages; when the workers asked their bosses why, they were told it was to pay for the Queen's jewels! They would be shown a picture of the Queen and told: "She has a crown, right? Okay, you came to Canada, pal. She's our Queen, right? Okay, you pay ten per cent." The poor labourer paid tax on his wages, and the employer who skimmed it from his paycheque paid nothing. It was unbelievable what went on. And this startling information came to me by simply talking to these men—it was that easy.

When I was a reporter in the 1960s, the approaches to gathering information were slightly different. It was novel to have women gathering information, for example, because women had never worked in this milieu. A newspaper might hire an actress to interview someone and have her wear a hidden "body pack" tape recorder. Bugging devices were also used. But today these approaches are obsolete; we live in a much more sophisticated age. There is a great body of information available that wasn't available then.

For example, if you want to research a company today, your starting point is to obtain a copy of its registration from the provincial Ministry of Consumer and Commercial Relations.* This gives you the address of the company and the names and addresses of its directors—information that is easily available to the public.

But don't think that a registration check spells out all the details and any wrongdoings of a company. And don't feel that because a company is registered with the government, the province has given it its blessing. Neither of these assumptions is true. The function of registration records is to give an address where the company's executives can be served with a summons in case of a lawsuit— that's all.

Author's note: Refer to Chapters 15, 16, and 17 on government sources for further information.

Here is a brief word on numbered companies: Some people believe that numbered companies are sinister, but the only reason there are numbered companies is that the English language wasn't keeping pace with incorporations. Business people were being prevented from forming companies, because they couldn't name them fast enough. Remember the old letter prefixes in our telephone numbers? Bell Canada changed from letter prefixes to numerical prefixes for reasons of efficiency.

It's easy to collect financial information on public companies. Their earnings are listed in several places, including the *Card Index*, published by The Financial Post's Corporation Service Group and available in the public library. Or you can call any brokerage house and ask for the information, saying that you're interested in buying shares in the company. Also, the public has access to provincial records in provincial securities commission files.

Another, often overlooked, source of information on companies is the municipality where they are located. Municipalities are revenue collectors and therefore keep all sorts of business licences or permits that you can ask to see. When companies file information with the provincial and federal governments, they usually have a lawyer fill out the forms carefully. But when they're filing information with a municipality, the owners of the company generally do so themselves and are much more open about their affairs.

Very few people ask to see another type of public record—tax assessment rolls. These are never more than five or six months out of date because, in Ontario at least, they're tied to the enumeration system for municipal elections. Tax assessment rolls are kept in city hall archives and are a great source when trying to locate a person or determine what a company's property is worth.

Court records can be beneficial as well. You can use them to discover if there are any judgments against an individual or a company, if an action was contested, and if there have been any bankruptcies.

Determining land ownership is easy enough to do. There are massive land registry systems in each province that the public can use to trace any piece of land back hundreds of years.

Gaining financial information on private companies is tricky, but there are a few sources that are helpful. When private companies borrow money, they have to first establish credibility; to do this, they usually co-operate with financial clearing houses. For a relatively small fee, you can check a company's credit rating, which, because records must be kept up-to-date, can yield a lot of information. There are various specialized clearing houses that provide this service; it depends on the industry you're investigating.

As you can see, there is in fact a lot of information on the public record; there's no need to stumble onto things the way we used to. When I was a reporter, there wasn't the record-keeping system that exists today. In a way, there's too much information available now. In order to get down to the bone, you have to discard 99 per cent of the information you obtain. It's really the 1 per cent you're after: the "why" of things. Everything else then falls into place.

Winning by Phone

Chapter Eight

The telephone can be the most effective means of finding information fast—provided that you get through to the proper person and that *you* are in control of the conversation. In the following edited interview, Dr. Gary S. Goodman, an internationally recognized telecommunications expert and President of Goodman Communications Corporation of Glendale, California, suggests ways of gaining and exercising that control by keeping notes, using positive, assertive phraseology, getting past secretaries, and making the most of conversations with prominent people.

Goodman is a former assistant professor of communications at the University of Southern California and has authored four books on effective telephone interviewing and telemarketing, including *Winning by Telephone.*

There are a number of rules I adhere to before I pick up the telephone. I first straighten out my entire calling environment. I like to take notes of every conversation, and an orderly desk lets me concentrate on the message. By taking notes, I know I'm not going to miss anything, and if I hear something that I want to come back to later, I can make a point of cuing myself on paper.

I start off by dividing a sheet of paper into four sections. In the upper left-hand section of the page, I list the statements I need to make during the conversation. In the upper right-hand section, I list my main questions. In the lower left-hand portion, I take notes of the conversation. In the remaining section, I jot down questions that come to mind during the conversation.

The purpose of this format is to keep me from losing any meaningful ideas. We've all had the experience of thinking of something brilliant when someone is saying something. But often, when we listen to them, we jump to the next thought and forget what that brilliant flash was.

I like to have enough pencils and paper handy so I can take notes. Sometimes I actually write out beforehand, word for word, how a conversation might unfold. I always know in advance the gist of what I'm going to say. This is necessary, because I have to use the proper phraseology in order to produce the response I'm looking for. We lose a lot of power by using the wrong kinds of words.

Let me illustrate this by pointing out what I call "weasel words." We are too civil. For instance, we say, "Would you kindly consider the prospect of speaking with me later on, maybe around, say, two o'clock or so?" What we have done, of course, is string together a litany of weasel words that cue the listener the wrong way. They ask the listener for some kind of commitment too early in the thought. When we ask for something using the words "Would you?", a red flag goes up in the listener's mind. The person thinks: "Oh, oh. This person's asking me for something. I'm going to take the conservative option and say 'No.'" During the remainder of the sentence that is requesting something, the listener is saying, "No, no, no, no, no." By the time we finish, they have built up a tremendous case for the negative.

Instead of doing that, I use *assumptive phraseology*. I assume the "yes" by saying: "What we'll do is this." or: "Let's do this." or even: "We'll set aside a time this afternoon, say five o'clock, and we'll talk then, okay?" By arranging my phraseology in this fashion—by making a conclusive statement and then throwing in an "okay?" at the end of it—I produce commitment. The key here, however, is the tone of my voice. The more important the thing I'm asking for, the lighter my tone of voice is. The content may be very assertive; on paper it may seem even strident, overly aggressive, or pushy. But it doesn't sound that way over the telephone if my tone is light.

I avoid a heavy tone of voice in most situations, unless I feel that my rights are being trampled on. If they are, I say something like this, very slowly: "I'm going to make something very clear." I'm not screaming; I'm simply saying it very slowly. It's almost like saying:

"Read my lips." The person thinks: "Oh, oh. Something heavy is coming." I'm being intense, but in a very restrained way. It's important to stay in control.

It helps to practise controlling your voice by speaking into a tape recorder and role-playing the conversation with yourself and other people; or you can read the newspaper into a tape recorder, using various tones of voice. This enables people to explore the range of expressiveness in their voices. Most of us have failed to cultivate our voices, because we don't listen and don't use our voices in a trained way.

I have a theory, although I have not yet substantiated it: People who are good singers are good listeners and good telephone communicators, because they can listen effectively and therefore modulate their voices to be harmonious with the voice of the person they're speaking to. That is probably the most important standard by which to assess the merit of someone's telephone tonal performance. It's important to echo the other person's voice. Echoing is a very important device for creating what some behavioural theorists call "consubstantiality." This term means creating a feeling that you are of the same substance as another person. A more casual way of terming it is "identification." Persuasion theorists believe that the number one factor in successful persuasion is a feeling of identification. We need to feel that we're like each other, or of the same kind, at least in certain critical ways. So your tone can create harmony, a feeling that you're talking with a brother or someone who comes from the same place you do.

Some people have asked me if there is a best time to reach people during the day. I think that people who are called late in the afternoon are receiving the subtle message that they are not top priority. Most of us have lists of things we want to accomplish during the day, and the bottom of the list are the things that get done at the very end of the day. I think most people are sensitive to that. So if you want to get the best reception, try to reach people as early as is practical in the morning. If you're trying to reach really, really important people, then try really, really early in the morning!

On the other hand, it can also pay to call late in the afternoon. By this time, the important people have likely sent their screeners home. So you find that a number of celebrities come to the telephone themselves.

Another problem area may be getting past secretaries. The first thing you have to do is "credential" yourself. There's a ritual at the beginning of a telephone conversation; let's examine it by role-playing for a moment. I'll open the conversation, while you pretend to be the secretary:

"Hello, is John there?"

"Who's calling, please?"

"Oh, this is Gary Goodman."

"Of which firm?"

"Oh, Goodman Communications."

"Does Mr. Miller know you're calling?"

"Well, no, not really."

"Well, can I tell him what it's about?"

"Sure, it's about our new book."

"One moment please...I'm sorry, Mr. Miller is in a meeting right now. Can I take your number and have him get back to you later?"

"Yes, okay."

That's exactly how a telephone conversation usually goes. However, the person who is receiving the call, the secretary, is schooled in a very narrow way in order to handle a certain spectrum of possible conversational paths. Now let's role-play again, with me opening the conversation:

"Hello. Long distance, Dr. Gary Goodman calling for John. Thank you."

"Uh, one moment please."

This approach works astronomically well. (If I wasn't calling long distance, I would simply drop the reference to it.) It works because it violates the expectations of the screener by telling her or him: "Look, I'm using a different tone. I'm open. I'm revealing information to you and doing all your work for you. You don't have to worry about asking me for information, because I've just given it to you."

What typically happens is that the screener isn't ready to listen; she or he is ready to ask questions instead. The person says, "Uh, what? I'm sorry, could you repeat that?"

I say, "Certainly," then talk very slowly: "Dr. Gary Goodman, Goodman Communications, long distance for John. Thank you very much." I punctuate it a little differently this time, with "thank you very much." The key here is that I'm revealing information. I give the secretary enough content to take to the person I want to speak to, and it sounds as if I've called the company before. The "thank you" part of my comment is in effect saying: "I don't want to hear any more from you." It's like working with a computer and sending something by electronic mail by hitting the "send" button.

Here's another variation on that call. Once again, I'll open the conversation, while you respond as the secretary:

"Hello. Gary Goodman for John. Thank you."

"Well, may I tell him what this is about?"

"Certainly. It's about our recent correspondence. Thank you very much."

"Well, maybe I could help you."

"I wish you could. But I'm sure he'll want to speak with me personally. Thank you again."

"Well, he asked me to take all of his calls, so maybe I could help you."

"Well, that's fine. What were your annual revenues last year?"

"Oh, gee, I don't know. You'll have to speak with John."

"Fine, I'll be happy to hold. Thank you."

If I encounter a comment like: "He's in a meeting," this is what I reply:

"That's fine. I appreciate that. How long do you expect he'll be in the meeting?"

"It's hard to say."

"I understand. Well, what I'll do is simply get back to him later. Oh, by the way—when's a better time, early in the morning or later in the afternoon?"

"Well, sometimes you can catch him in the morning."

"Around seven?"

"Oh no, he's not in then. Try around seven-thirty, that's when he's in."

"Fine. I'll call him then. Thanks so much. 'Bye."

It's also a good idea to sound prominent yourself. The title of your company or organization can promise a benefit to the person you're calling. Use the highest possible credential. It can be even more advantageous if you're a member of the press. You can start publishing a little newsletter, even periodically, and that way you can call up and say, "Hello. Dr. Gary Goodman with the Telephone Effectiveness Newsletter calling for John's comment. Thank you." Wow, will you get through! You've become the power of the press, and there are all kinds of positive things associated with that. It also helps to announce yourself slowly; important people always announce themselves slowly. Let your opening drop like 20-pound weights. I make the person hang on every word—it allows me to control the call, and it gets the jump on the other person. Either you control, or you are controlled. And it all takes place right at the beginning of the call.

Here's another very effective technique to use with secretaries. Let's say I have already asked for John. The secretary is the first person speaking:

"May I take a message?"

"Certainly. Do you expect he'll be calling back tomorrow morning?"

"I'm not certain if he will."

In this way I have got the secretary to answer my question. I promised her that I would leave the message, but then I didn't. What most people want is some momentary sign of reassurance that they're getting their way, so we should agree with them and then go right back to where we were. They're totally unprepared for this. What we're doing is saying: "You're in charge. Everything's fine. You're getting your way." But we're mis-cuing the person—it works like magic.

There are some people who are uncomfortable saying anything important over the telephone. To overcome this, I suggest you develop a new technique to disarm them. Start the conversation by acknowledging that some people have difficulty speaking comfortably over the telephone. Because most prominent people are concerned that their comments might in some way be changed or misrepresented, continue by saying: "I want to put your concerns about this to rest, because it's my intention, before we say good-bye, to repeat to you the gist of what I have understood you to say. And if there are any corrections, you can make them then." I am thus giving the person what appears to be a privilege of censorship, or at least some modification, over the material.

Here is another type of problem: If you are a journalist interviewing a politician, and you encounter a "No comment" response, probe a little further:

"Well, may I ask why you might be reluctant to comment on that?"

The person may say, "I don't have any comment to make on that, either."

I then say, "I appreciate that, but it might be said that the reason you are reluctant to comment is because of such-and-such. Is that a fair thing to say?"

I'm probing and rephrasing and restating. But I'm constantly coming back in for the kill.

If the politician were to say, "I'm too busy to speak with you," I would reply:

"I appreciate that. I'm busy, too. However, this will just take a 'ent or two."

..er all, who isn't busy? If you aren't busy, then you're a bozo—that's the way it works in our culture. So when people say to me, "I'm busy," good for them. They're probably gainfully doing something. But so am I. They're also trying to raise themselves above me. So I say very nicely and quickly, "So am I. I'll just make this brief." I don't ask, "May I ask you a question?" I just say, "I'll make this brief," and in a light tone of voice I add, "Just a quick question or two." Then I ask my questions.

Another way of controlling your conversations is by pausing in the middle of sentences. By doing this, you speak longer than the other person would normally tolerate, and you do so without bringing attention to what you are doing. It also precludes another person from interrupting you. When most of us were taught to read aloud in classrooms, we were taught to pause at the ends of sentences. So when we pause in the middle of a sentence, the person knows that we have a lot more ground to cover. As a result, the person listens more attentively and wonders, "What is he or she going to say next?"

Properly used, the telephone is a fantastic medium, but it's undervalued. Many people are not fully aware of just how valuable it can be, even to comparison-shop. I remember shopping for a new car a few years ago. I found the model number I wanted, the colour, and the other features. I telephoned one dealer and was told that the car I wanted sold for $18,000. This is how the conversation went:

"Oh, that's too high," I began.

"What do you mean, too high? You're not going to find this car anywhere else at a cheaper price."

"Well, as a matter of fact, I *have* found it somewhere else, and they're asking about fifteen hundred dollars less than you are."

"You don't mean the car over at Alhambra Porsche-Audi, do you?"

"Exactly."

"You wouldn't want that car."

"Why not?"

"Because it has about eighty-five miles on it."

"That doesn't bother me."

So what did I do? I promptly called Alhambra and inquired about the car. I ended up buying from them, saving myself $1,500. And I didn't know the car existed before that person blew it. I was using the power of competition and doing it by telephone. Consumers can do that for any item.

"Famous Last Words"

Chapter Nine

Timothy Findley's novels are meticulously researched. Even his publisher's lawyers admit to having difficulty determining where fact ends and fiction begins.

Famous Last Words, Findley's fourth and most exhaustively prepared book, required four years of research. A gripping account of fascism during the Second World War, the novel probes an international cabal whose members include the Duke and Duchess of Windsor, prominent Nazis, and other well-known figures. The narrator is Hugh Mauberley, a fictitious figure borrowed from one of Ezra Pound's poems. Mauberley is an American expatriate writer who is a confidant of members of the cabal. He knows too much, flees the Nazis, hides in an Austrian hotel, and scrawls everything he knows in silver pencil along the walls of the hotel. He is murdered while doing this, and the story really unfolds by flashing back to his handwritten account.

In the following interview, Findley reveals how relatively simple the research was for this complex novel.

At a writer's conference, I had a wonderful talk with the author E. L. Doctorow. He wrote what I would call the definitive megafiction book, *Ragtime*. When I asked him how he did his research, he answered this way: "I discovered that once I had really stated my subject, I became a magnet." That is a very good definition of what happens when you have staked out your territory. Doctorow's territory was pre-First World War. My territory was 1943 back to wherever it was going to lead as far as the Duke and Duchess of Windsor were concerned.

The magnet phenomenon works as follows: You pick up a book of basic history, you read, and you discover a sequence of names. Let us pretend that Doctorow and I have picked up the same book. Doctorow does not write or think like me, and I do not write or think like him; therefore, he and I are not going to follow the same line in reading this book. As Doctorow reads—and this is the magnet at work—his eye hits on a particular sequence, and he follows it. He picks up on names, personality traits, the recurrence of links between people and events. A whole other set of magnetic episodes are going to happen with me.

My subject dictated a sequence that followed fascist thinking from one set of people to another. I had to begin with something basic, so I used W. L. Shirer's *Rise and Fall of the Third Reich*—an invaluable guide to fascism and the Second World War. Where did it take me? For one thing, its bibliography gave me a reading list. I discovered an alarming consistency in the cast of characters from one piece of reading to another. Here's a good example: In one book I discovered that the wedding of the Duke and Duchess of Windsor had taken place at the Château de Conde in France, which was owned by a man named Charles Eugène Bedaux. The information was a mere mention of the wedding—just a sentence—but I had never heard of Bedaux and was intrigued. In another book, however, I had read that the Duchess was at a villa in the south of France at the time, and the Duke was in Austria. That led to this question: "Why did they get married at Bedaux's villa, when they could have been married where they already had friends whom they knew were willing to perform the ceremony?"

Reading newspaper accounts of the wedding, I learned that Bedaux had offered the Windsors his villa absolutely out of the blue—he did not even know them. And I still knew very little about him; he was a mystery and a challenge. What helped me understand this man was a series of columns written by Janet Flanner in the *New Yorker*. Sure enough, my instinct had been correct: I had made the right connection, and Bedaux had been worth tracking, because it turned out that he had been pivotal to the Windsors' fascist connections.

Bedaux was the inventor of the concept of *time study*. He would walk into factories and say, "Get rid of those people—they're stopping you. Bring in other people and make use of them." He worked out a system that to me is highly fascist: He would extract the most from labourers, making them work very hard for four minutes, then relax for one minute. In other words, he advocated turning people into machines to make them more productive. The carrot to reward them was the one minute of rest. He made a fortune. And, not incidentally, some Canadian firms adopted his methods.

I read through all the books I could find on the Windsors to discover any further connections with Bedaux. I had to do a lot of scrutinizing, because some books were very sympathetic and others were overly damning. A good researcher has to learn to recognize an author's bias.

The real starting point for me was to determine what was to be the circle of events and who were to be the people involved in this cabal I was imagining—and then had begun to discover might have been real. By reading through material I had borrowed from libraries and purchased at bookstores, I discovered that at its widest, the circle included people like Ezra Pound, the Duke and Duchess of Windsor, Bedaux, Walter Schellenberg (who was the top SS counter-intelligence officer), Ribbentrop, and Rudolf Hess. The magnet in me took over once I had that overview. As soon as I saw any of those names, I would mentally reach out to collect data. I could be walking down the street and out of the corner of my eye see Hess's face staring out of a bookstore window from the dust jacket of a book. It's an eclectic process.

I also read the *bibliographies* of every book and followed them up, ultimately reading nearly everything written about some of these key figures. By reading and rereading material I acquired, over time, a deeper understanding of the characters I had found.

Another thing that paid off for me was to tell friends what I was writing about. One of these friends, the writer Charles Taylor, was especially helpful. His father, E. P. Taylor, lives in Nassau, and the Taylors inevitably got to know some of the people in the circle around the Duke of Windsor during his tenure there as governor during the Second World War. This connection turned out to be invaluable for me. In my novel I used a real-life incident involving Sydney Oakes and his father, Sir Harry Oakes, but I gave my own interpretation of the circumstances in which it had taken place. It is a pertinent scene that develops the character of Sir Harry and, I think, forms a part, however small, of the explanation of why he was murdered.

When I had finished *Famous Last Words*, the lawyers for my publisher, Clarke Irwin, were worried that Sydney might still be alive and sue. My memory told me he had died in a car accident. Charles Taylor helped me confirm this by telephoning his father's secretary in Nassau. The secretary made a few calls to relatives of the Oakeses, who confirmed that, indeed, he was dead.

There were other areas where Charles Taylor helped me. A number of places mentioned in my book—Spain, Vienna, Rome, Venice, and Nassau—were places I had never been. Quite deliberately, I avoided visiting them, because I wanted to maintain a kind of mythic view of them, so that they would be "written" places, not real. I read a lot about them and asked a lot of questions. For instance, I mentioned to Charles Taylor that I had placed the governor's mansion in Nassau at the top of a hill. He remarked, "Yes, it's at the top of a sort of hill. It's actually just a slight rise in the land." He was greatly amused. I also asked him other questions: "What do the trees smell like?" "What does the land smell like at night?" By researching the setting in this way, I was getting a mythic, distanced, very "writerly" interpretation of the place. Don't forget: The book was being written by a writer, Mauberley, who was a failed romantic. I had to serve his style.

I also studied maps in the library to get the geography and street connections right. Studying photographs was also helpful to make sure I was correctly describing the clothing, cars, and things like that. These were the kinds of details Mauberley thrived on: dress, appearance, atmosphere.

This process is, of course, different than a journalistic reportage of a place. That is a valid type of approach, but it would destroy a book like mine, which requires a different kind of shape to make it succeed.

I didn't do all the research in one fell swoop. I would research, then write, then repeat the process. I might suddenly say to myself, "Okay, now I need everything I can get about Ezra Pound," then plunge into that and place the material into my Pound file.

I used four filing boxes for my novel, each of them measuring two-and-a-half-feet deep. I would file material under names, places, clothing, photographic material, and songs.

Songs were very important. I had to find the words to various songs, and it's not as easy as it might appear. There is a moment in *Famous Last Words* when Edward and Mrs. Simpson are experiencing the sort of romance where they have to hold hands under the table. They couldn't touch one another openly, because the whole world was staring. I thought it was appropriate to have music in the background that would recreate the atmosphere of this scene. I cross-referenced songs at a special library at the Canadian Broadcasting Corporation and came up with Jerome Kern's 1936 hit, "A Fine Romance," with the words: "...A fine romance, my friend, this is; a fine romance, with no kisses..." Perfect.

I never made a trip to the reference library in Toronto to research just one point. I would make a list of ten points to research, and this made the trip worthwhile.

You have to be very careful when you research a novel. I made a few embarrassing mistakes. For one thing, I created a non-existent rank in the Royal Air Force. Somebody picked it up early enough, so that by the time the book was published in the United States, it had been corrected.

Here's a story to explain how I could have avoided a few other major errors. Every year in mid-August, I visit a wonderful old hotel along the coast of Maine. Some very interesting people stay there. On this particular visit, I met an Englishwoman, Diana Marler, and told her about my novel, which was then in progress. She told me that her best friend was the daughter of Sir Edward Peacock, who had been the Duke of Windsor's lawyer. Diana even had a desk that Peacock had once owned and that the Duke himself had used when signing legal papers.

I lent Diana all of the manuscript dealing with Ned Allenby, whom I had created as the British Undersecretary of State for Foreign Affairs. The Allenby home is set in Kent, England, where Charles Lindbergh turns up and Allenby is murdered. I had, in fact, made Allenby up by modelling him on a conglomerate of several people, some of them well known. The portrait of Allenby was apparently so effective that people told me after they had read the book that they had known him! Some had even known him "very well."

Diana Marler told me she had found two *glaring* mistakes. I was alarmed. The first one was this: I had written about a gardener in one scene, pushing a wheelbarrow full of dead marigolds. She pointed out that people of Allenby's station would never have grown marigolds—marigolds were "cottage" flowers. My flowers would have to be something else, like roses. That may sound silly, but it was terribly important. The garden had to be right; it was key material.

She also pointed out where I had used an improper phrase. In the scene where Lindbergh is trying to sell Allenby on fascism and the Nazis, Allenby becomes so angry that he says: "I don't want to hear about this, you goddamn son of a bitch." Diana said Allenby would never have used the term "son of a bitch." He might have called Lindbergh a bloody idiot, or a bastard, but no Englishman of that class would have used the North American term I had given him. Like a fool I said, "Thank you, Diana. I'll think about that." I thought that "bastard" wasn't strong enough and left my original term in.

I shouldn't have. A dozen people have come up to me since the book was published and told me, "I really loved the book, but —in *England*—why did Ned Allenby call Lindbergh a son of a bitch? He would never have said that." Readers pick up on these things, and Diana was right. It sounds almost trite, but, you see, it isn't; using the wrong phrase destroyed the veracity of that scene.

The lesson here is that you have to learn to be a good listener. Your will has to bow to the research, and you have to accommodate information. I didn't, and it had a jarring effect on a significant number of readers. They lost the thread of the moment when they read that sentence and thought, "Oh, that's wrong!"

Coming back to where I began: The personality searching for any given information dictates how that research proceeds. If you handed five writers the same subject and said, "All five of you are going to research and write about this topic," they would write five totally different books. This is so because each writer has his or her own magnet, a completely unique way of interpreting things, guided by personal imagination.

Fighting Back
Chapter Ten

Dave Mackenzie is one of two union organizers who played an instrumental role in the election of Canada's Lynn Williams to the presidency of the powerful United Steelworkers of America. The vote, taken in March, 1984, was a milestone in Canadian labour history. It was the first time a Canadian had been elected president of the 750,000-member union, 80 per cent of whose members are Americans. Williams personally asked Mackenzie to help organize his Canadian campaign. The results speak for themselves: Williams won 93.5 per cent of the votes cast in Canada, even though the director of Canada's largest Steelworker district, Dave Patterson, backed Williams's opponent.

Mackenzie was no stranger to organizing union campaigns. A former field organizer for the New Democratic Party, he had played a key role in two major Steelworker strikes—one against Radio Shack in 1979, the other against Irwin Toy in 1981. In this edited interview Mackenzie, who now works as a national organizer for the Steelworkers, discusses how he gathered information for these events. Make no mistake about it: Information was the critical factor at each step. Again, notice how the research principles employed here may be used in many other situations.

There are certain standard tools that any union organizer requires for researching purposes. One is the Scott's manufacturing and industrial catalogues, which are a sort of industrial version of the Yellow Pages, published by a division of Southam Communications Limited and available at most public libraries. They are published for entire provinces as well as for individual cities. They are valuable because they provide a complete listing of every manufacturing and industrial company in an area. The companies are listed by street and region, along with a capsule summary of their structure—where head office is, who the chief executive officers are, and, most important, how many employees work there.

For example, if one was interested in locating non-unionized plants in one section of Toronto, one would consult the Scott's directory for Toronto, which lists all existing companies in that city. Then it would be a matter of telephoning the special library at the Ontario Ministry of Labour to find out which companies were unionized. This library has a complete printout of every collective bargaining agreement in the province.

The other way of ascertaining if a company is unionized is to call the firm directly and ask. Once you know that a company isn't unionized and has enough employees to make an organizing drive worthwhile, then the organizing can begin.

In order to learn about the working conditions in a plant, we might go directly to the plant and hand out leaflets when the employees come to work and when they leave. This is a standard leaflet with an introduction to the benefits of belonging to a union, a list of the employees' legal rights, and with a tear-off section that they can send back to us. In the vast majority of cases, we don't get any feedback. It depends on the work force and the conditions. If we hand out leaflets at a dozen plants and a total of four workers reply, we are doing well. Sometimes a leaflet sits in a worker's locker for years, and suddenly he becomes angry with the company and calls us. What we're really doing by "leafletting" is planting seeds. Eventually a storm brews. I follow up on all calls, no matter how dim the prospects of an organizing drive might appear. This is the only way to establish that vital human contact.

One thing I've found useful is to make contact with social service and cultural agencies that have contact with ethnic communities. Sometimes we go through a central labour body, and sometimes we use the telephone book and call ethnic groups directly. We make this contact because the work force in Canada is rapidly changing. A lot of newly arrived immigrants work in manufacturing plants and are not organized, so we spend a lot of time talking to them to research the demography and ethnic background of the employees in various plants. After all, it's no good standing outside a plant handing out leaflets in English if 80 per cent of the work force is Portuguese.

Another reason we make these contacts is that we learn about Workers' Compensation cases. By talking with one or two workers who have been involved in such cases, we learn about specific issues and grievances that we then address in our leaflets.

The supporting staff of local politicians can also be useful by supplying information about minority groups. Sometimes the staff receives a cluster of complaints from workers in certain industries, and this can alert us to particular issues.

A union organizer's most valuable tool, however, is a list of employees at any one plant, because then it is possible to make individual house calls. There are a variety of ways of obtaining such a list. Plants that don't want a union to form try very hard to keep these lists to themselves, so a union organizer tries to develop a friendly contact within the plant's office staff. It can be a painstaking process, but if we establish five contacts, it is often the case that one of them, indirectly, knows someone who works in the personnel department. With that contact, a payroll list can be photocopied and anonymously sent to the union.

The other way to obtain a list is to write down the licence plate numbers of the cars in the company's parking lot. Through the provincial Ministry of Transportation, and for a nominal fee, we can trace the names and addresses of the car owners. Contacting these workers gives us a lot of information about the working conditions of a company, which helps to make an organizing drive easier.

Allow me to say something about major organizing drives. The 1979 strike at Radio Shack had a profound influence in Ontario. At that time, Ontario did not have automatic dues check-offs (automatic payroll deductions for union dues) for plants that were organized. Until then an employer knew who supported the union and could therefore discriminate against those workers. The Radio Shack strike forced the government to make laws that could prevent that kind of situation. The strike also showed up a classic case of discrimination against women, because a majority of the workers were women, and it was clear that they were being treated with contempt.

I became involved in the strike a month after it had been launched. My job was to work with a boycott campaign that the Steelworkers had decided to pursue. A boycott is a technique that can be used only in a limited number of cases. In this instance it was very effective, because Radio Shack sold a number of high-profile products.

The boycott was also effective because the company has many franchise outlets, which were an easy target. We concentrated the boycott on outlets in large shopping centres and small towns. We ran picket lines in stores across the country. We didn't prevent customers from entering the stores, but we handed out our literature outlining the background of the boycott. By using this approach, we forced some stores to close temporarily.

Radio Shack, we learned through its literature, was part of the multinational, American-based Tandy Corporation. We wrote anonymously to the company and received its annual report. This gave us a list of all the other companies associated with Radio Shack.

For the boycott to be successful, we had to enlist the support of other unions in towns and cities where the Steelworkers weren't represented. To do this, we first had to draw up a list of places where Radio Shack had stores. This was easily done after reading the company's product catalogues. Then it was a matter of matching those places where the Steelworkers were represented and those where we weren't. The central labour body in Canada, the Canadian Labour Congress, gave us a list of unions active in the localities where we weren't, and we contacted them.

One tough question for us to research was: What group would boycott Radio Shack's products? By visiting various stores and studying the product catalogues, it was obvious that the main products sold were stereo equipment, radios, and, most recently, video games, and from watching the people in the stores, we realized that the main market for these goods was teenagers.

Once we had determined that, the question became: How can we reach the teenage market with information that will help the boycott? The obvious answer was: through teachers, who encounter that group every day. So we established strong links with some teachers' organizations.

But we did not limit our information campaign to students. We researched the Tandy Corporation through the U.S. Securities Exchange Commission and learned that the company's annual shareholders' meeting was being held in Fort Worth, Texas. We contacted the local office of the Steelworkers in Forth Worth and arranged for union members to picket the annual meeting. That action got good media coverage for the Radio Shack strike.

Another interesting development in the strike was that a spy, who had been hired by Radio Shack to infiltrate us, suddenly came to our defence. Evidently his spying activities had bothered his conscience. We had suspected he was a spy but hadn't done any research to verify it. What you can do today, however, is contact any number of provincial licensing bodies to find out if a person is a registered private investigator. In Ontario it's the Ontario Provincial Police.

Our experience with the Radio Shack strike was important because it involved many crucial issues: women's rights, labour reform, and the multinational control of the Canadian economy. It also helped us win the support and involvement of a lot of other groups. This initial success went a long way for us. When we launched a similar boycott against the Irwin Toy Company in 1981, we already had a list of people outside our union who could help us.

During that boycott, the kinds of information and the ways we obtained it were similar to the techniques we had used with Radio Shack. We discovered a lot of company information in Irwin Toy's own product catalogues. They told us, for example, that Irwin was an umbrella company that embraced many brand names. We also learned that Irwin's Canadian distributor was Atari, one of the largest distributors of video games. This information made it easy for us to name specific toys we wanted to boycott and to identify the group that purchased the greatest amount of them.

Our boycott unquestionably had an impact: Irwin soon settled with us. We had successfully picketed their stores and distributed literature giving us a high public profile. It must have hurt Irwin's image, and the company was no doubt afraid that the public would remember it as an employer who treated its employees unfairly and as a union buster.

Gathering information on the organizing drive to have Lynn Williams elected as president of the Steelworkers required a different approach than the cases I've mentioned. First of all, one is largely constrained by the rules and regulations that the union sets down. The Steelworkers are different than most unions in that every member can vote. Each local work place is a polling station. Other unions usually hold conventions, and only a limited number of representatives can vote. And the Steelworkers do not, for example, permit candidates to use union facilities in any way; they must rent their own facilities.

In this campaign we assembled lists of workers who had been sympathetic to Williams in previous elections. I had personally kept lists from previous campaigns. Keeping such records is vital. So we were able to contact these previous supporters and persuade them to nominate Williams.

The head office of our international union helped us indirectly by providing both candidates with a computerized printout of which locals had voted for which candidate and what percentage of the workers in each local had actually voted. This told us more precisely where our strengths and weaknesses lay and which locals required more of our energies.

Naturally, we wanted to get Williams as much media publicity as possible. We arranged to have him visit the locals where most of our members resided in order to do media interviews. We used the *Canadian Advertising Rates and Data*, published by Maclean Hunter, to obtain a list of all media outlets across the country.

Finally, we did a lot of what we call "plant-gating": Those workers who supported us handed out literature to other Steelworkers within their plants. Overall, our approach worked very well.

Library Research
Made Easy
Chapter Eleven

Brian Land is one of Canada's most outstanding librarians. He headed a branch of the Windsor Public Library before becoming an executive assistant to the federal Minister of Finance in 1963. He has been a professor of the Faculty of Library Science at the University of Toronto and its Dean, as well as the president of the Canadian Library Association. The author of an invaluable research tool, *Directory of Associations in Canada*, Land has been the director of the Ontario Legislative Library Research and Information Services since 1978.

In this account he discusses basic approaches to using libraries in Canada.

The first thing for a researcher to do is to identify, as closely as possible, what the problem is. Most library users are notoriously vague about what they want, so they must first understand what the search is supposed to accomplish. To achieve this, it is helpful to find out what the application or context of the information might be; one way to do this is to narrow down the geographical area of the search. For example, if information on gardening is requested, the geographical aspect is especially important, because information must be appropriately selected for different terrains. The time frame of the material you seek is another way to refine questions.

It is useful to skim through a book, article, or a library's clipping file on a subject to gain an overview of your material. This process may make you change the direction of your research, because as you learn something about the subject in general, you may become fascinated with certain aspects. This approach also helps you refine and define your questions.

It helps to distinguish between the different kinds of information available. A student writing a high school paper might find an essay in an encyclopedia an appropriate source. On the other hand, someone preparing an article for a learned journal would require academic sources as opposed to more popular information.

Indexes are extremely valuable in any kind of library research, and yet I have found that even first-year university students are unaware of the most standard indexes. The most basic indexes in our country are the *Canadian Periodical Index*, the *Canadian News Index*, the *Canadian Business Index*, and the *Microlog Index*. They cover most Canadian newspapers, magazines, journals, and government and business reports.*

Indexes are being offered increasingly through on-line computer services. But computerization really only started in the late 1960s, which means that you still have to do manual index searches if you wish to locate publications before this period. There are directories that tell you if a particular publication has been indexed, the most notable of which is *Ulrich's International Periodicals Directory*, which covers Canadian publications. Also, local community libraries often undertake the tedious process of indexing their home town papers.

Once you have pinpointed the journal, magazine, or newspaper you want, there is still the task of locating it. Several directories of libraries make it easier for you. There is the *Canadian Library Handbook*, published by Micromedia Limited, and the *American Library Directory*, which, despite its title, has a Canadian section. It goes into a lot of detail, listing the number of volumes in a library and the library's book budget. The American directory gives the size of each library, so the researcher has an idea of the likelihood of finding a publication or serial in a given library.

Here's another tip for locating publications in the public library system: Look for "union lists." A union list has nothing to do with trade unions but is a directory of libraries that hold particular

---

Author's note: These sources are discussed in more depth in Chapter 14, "Using Libraries in Canada."

journals. For example, the public libraries in Toronto band together every two years to produce the *Guide to Periodicals and Newspapers in the Public Libraries of Metropolitan Toronto*. So if you were researching the pulp and paper industry in Canada, for instance, you could use this directory to learn what serialized publications cover that topic, where to find them, and how far back the copies are kept in that library. There is also a massive union list issued by the National Library of Canada, called *Union List of Serials in the Social Sciences and Humanities Held by Canadian Libraries*. Also, the National Research Council publishes the *Union List of Scientific Serials in Canadian Libraries*.

Let's come back to a point I made earlier on local libraries. Don't think that small local libraries are inefficiently equipped to handle serious research projects. All libraries in Canada are linked together in formal or informal networks. If you went into a library in a small town, and its resources were not sufficient, that library could borrow the necessary material for you from a larger city library through an interlibrary loan. So there's a sort of ripple effect at work, from the small to medium to large libraries; small libraries are not shut out of the network.

Also, keep in mind that when you're doing research involving a small town or region, the local library has a lot of geographical, historical, and political material in various forms that might not be readily available in larger libraries (although you can, of course, arrange an interlibrary loan from a larger library).

Sometimes "special libraries" can be of assistance. These are libraries outside the public library system, to which the public can often gain access for serious research purposes when the sources are not available in the public library system. For example, let us say that you are researching an aspect of forestry and require a specialized journal that isn't available in the public library. The special forestry library at a university will probably keep that journal.

There are directories of special libraries for various regions in Canada. You can locate the associations that represent special libraries and publish these directories by checking the *Directory of Associations in Canada*. These associations sell their directories, although most public libraries have them on file.

Some special libraries have very small physical book collections; they usually have periodicals and reports, but their main tools are the telephone and computer terminal. Rather than operating a library in the traditional sense, special librarians often use a computer to identify what documents are available and then, by telephone, locate where the documents are. There are networks of special librarians, particularly where there is a subject affinity. They are in competition with each other, but they share the professional understanding that they assist each other to locate and lend materials and to advise on how to access information.

Another timesaver is to talk with a librarian who specializes in a particular area. You can often glean an enormous amount of information this way before you even start on a research project.

If you can't locate the information you need in a public or special library, ask the head librarian of a department for the name of an expert in the area you're researching. Head librarians can be extremely valuable sources for locating unusual experts. You can also refer, once again, to the *Directory of Associations in Canada*, which lists hundreds of organizations from coast to coast. They can either help you themselves or direct you to the appropriate source.

The Science of Research

Chapter Twelve

In the international scientific community, Dr. Louis Siminovitch is a well-known figure. He is Geneticist-in-Chief at Toronto's Hospital for Sick Children, the Director of Research at Mount Sinai Hospital in Toronto, a senior scientist at the Ontario Cancer Institute, President of the National Cancer Institute, and a professor in and Chairman of the Department of Medical Genetics at the University of Toronto.

Dr. Siminovitch holds 17 prestigious honours and awards, including Officer of the Order of Canada. The author of 179 major scientific articles and papers, he is currently on the editorial board of 10 medical journals.

Although research in the sciences is in many ways different than gathering information in the humanities, there are a number of overlapping techniques. In this interview, Dr. Siminovitch reveals that the simple use of a network of information, such as telephone consultations with colleagues, can yield information that has a profound effect on the medical world. Literature searches, familiar to us in other contexts, also play a significant role.

Research in the sciences starts with an idea, something that you're interested in. Your idea is based on your knowledge of the existing literature. You know what the state of the art is, and you ask yourself: "What is the next important question that I have to address?" "Do I have the capacity to address this question?"

If you don't have the expertise, you must ask yourself whether or not you can acquire the knowledge easily. You don't want to formulate a trivial question, but rather one that is as important as possible. But you're always torn between the risky project and the one that is most likely to produce answers. This is because in order to be funded in science, you have to be able to show that you've produced something over a period of two to three years. These are the thought processes you go through. So sometimes you don't end up where you started.

There are two kinds of science. One is observational science, where you look at things. The other is where you say to yourself: "I have an idea that this is the way that this particular thing works. I'm going to see if I can show that that is in fact the way it works." This is what I call "Cartesian reasoning." You're really going from A to B to C, in a very logical progression, and asking questions all the time. This second kind of science is what I practise. Also, I'm always asking a fairly well-defined question.

You're best off if you're in close contact with experts—to use the cliché, "in the network." A lot of information, some of it unpublished, surfaces at meetings. So your personality is important, because you have to be able to communicate easily with people.

Research in the sciences differs greatly from that in other disciplines. What scientists do in their work is to uncover what is already there—nature or, if you will, the absolute truth. In the humanities, researchers are creating and/or interpreting data as they see fit.

The starting point in the sciences, especially if you know little about a given field, is to do a systematic literature search. Today this can be done by computer, although many scientific publications are not yet indexed or abstracted on computer files. You should not only read the articles but also look for footnotes and bibliographies and follow up on them.

I get a lot of my information over the telephone. Telephone bills for scientists have gone up astronomically lately. I may be talking with a colleague, and she may tell me about someone who has just researched a new clone or come up with a new development in cancer research. Sometimes I just tell a colleague over the phone that I'm researching a particular problem and ask if he knows of anyone doing similar work.

My daughter, for instance, wanted to start researching a scientific project, but no articles had been published on the topic. She wanted to find out as much about this area as possible before she began her research, so she telephoned four scientists to find out if anyone in the network had done anything on the topic. Scientists work within a community, and each of us recognizes who the expert is in an area. This is especially true in larger cities. In Boston, for example, the details of an experiment are known within two days after it has begun, because there are so many scientists in the network, and everyone keeps up-to-date.

Another valuable source for me comes from applications for grants. Scientists sometimes ask me to referee their project, and they provide me with all the published articles and reports on that topic.

And, believe it or not, scientists sometimes obtain information from reading newspapers. I recently read in the newspaper about research that is being conducted in England into a cancer gene— four weeks before the medical journals picked it up!

A Legal Approach
Chapter Thirteen

When it comes to libel and slander law, many Canadian magazines and newspapers choose to consult with lawyer Julian Porter. In 20 years of practice, Porter has established himself as one of the most capable—and controversial—lawyers in the country. One might think that this Queen's Counsel's methods of research are sophisticated and difficult to master. But Porter, like many of the other specialists in this book, actually uses down-to-earth approaches to assembling information. He prefers to observe things first-hand, interview his clients directly, read original documents himself, and consult with experts to see if he's on the right track. It's a formula that evidently works well for him. Here he recounts a few of his more memorable cases.

Facts, and how you present them, determine the outcome of a lawsuit. I prefer to use the old-fashioned way of gathering facts. I talk to a witness myself, before he or she testifies. A junior lawyer might not follow up on the little avenues in a conversation that can lead to a goldmine of information. Someone who is less experienced than me might not recognize the significance of what otherwise might be just a tiny little fact.

You really have to do primary research to establish the facts. All lawyers say that the facts are already there, but the truth of the matter is that the facts are how you arrange them. Keep in mind that a jury trial is a moving opera. There is a series of facts on a piece of paper, and there are five different lawyers presenting these facts with five totally different impressions. It all comes down to how you've conducted your initial interviews and assembled your information. In court, part of your job is to stay away from asking questions that can hurt your client.

When I interview my client before the trial takes place, I always ask, "Is there anything else that I've left out?" Or: "Anything I should ask?" Or: "Anything you want to ask me?" Open-ended questions like these are often very important and yield interesting information. I take a brutal approach with my client, much worse than an interrogation. This is the only way to prepare the person for the trial. On the other hand, when I interview a witness before a trial takes place, I usually take a soft approach.

I learned an important lesson in research when I was acting as an assistant crown prosecutor in a large tax evasion case, a case that became known as "The Great Sweet Grass Scandal." The case involved a series of interlocking companies whose shares were shuffled around and sold at inflated prices. The guilty party pretended the profits were going to outside purchasers, but he was eventually charged and convicted of tax evasion.

In this case Walter Williston, the senior prosecutor, taught me to personally examine all documents in the *original*—not the photocopies—because you miss any markings that may be on the backs of the originals. There were about 100,000 pieces of paper involved in this case, and I looked at all of them over a one-and-a-half-year period, then drew my conclusions. I could sense that the minutes had been redone. Some of the minutes and daily deposit books had been typed on a machine that had a broken letter "t." Typewriter experts studied the documents, and we were able to prove that two typewriters had been used. This took a lot of time to sort out, but this was a scam, meant to confuse anyone looking into it.

Young lawyers frantically read the law in their field. When you get older, however, you rely more on your own judgment. I now understand the basis of the law and usually ask a junior to look up existing cases for me. This can be done by using various indexes. I read and reread the cases to prepare myself. It pays to work with another person on the research, because that person may have a different point of view on a matter. He or she may well be right, and I may be wrong.

Sometimes a computer can help you do research. I once acted for Canadian artist Michael Snow, who was suing Eaton's because the company had attached red ribbons to his sculptured geese (which hang in downtown Toronto's Eaton Centre) as part of their Christmas decorations. This was an infringement of Section 14 of the Copyright Act. There weren't any reported decisions on this section. My junior, however, did a computer search at the Osgoode Hall law library and turned up one unreported case. I also learned of a lawyer who had written a paper on that section of the act, and in that paper there was mention of another unreported case. To round off our research, we looked through European law books to find cases that discussed how the issue was dealt with outside Canada.

It can help to do some research on the judge and the opposing lawyer. This information can help me decide how to present my case. It's important to know in advance who the judge is going to be. I try to ascertain what he or she knows about the law in my field. If, for instance, the judge is an expert on libel and slander, when I stand up in court I get right to the point immediately, stating what the issues are. But if the judge isn't well versed in that area of law, I first set out the principles and try to persuade the judge in a more subtle way. There are books available on the background of judges, but at this point in my career I usually know most of their backgrounds.

The same is true of lawyers, and if I'm unfamiliar with a lawyer I quickly try to learn if the person is clever. I'm not saying that *I'm* all that smart, but it makes a considerable difference if you're organizing a case with a lawyer who is either not as bright as you or who is a lot brighter than you. In court you throw out information, assuming that the other lawyer is taking it and running with it in a certain way. If the two of you are not on the same wave length, one of you is going to miss the boat.

I can tell a lot about the other lawyer just by the statement of claim he files, outlining his defence. This tells me right away if he knows his law or not. I also learn something if there is trouble setting a date for the legal proceedings. If the other lawyer is too busy or blames her secretary, this tells me something about her competence.

During the actual examination for discovery, when both sides present arguments for taking the matter before a court, I usually look at the way the lawyer organizes his papers. If they're scattered across the desk in a sloppy fashion, this may indicate he is confused. Thus, personal observations can be useful. Finally, if it's necessary to supplement this information, I may ask colleagues about the lawyer.

By the time the trial takes place, I can tell if I can get away with a few things during cross-examination. I may realize that the other lawyer doesn't have all the necessary papers at her fingertips, so I may be able to make statements that she can't dispute without a copy of the paper I have in front of me. Also, I may be able to pose a few leading questions to my witness without the other lawyer catching on. All of this may be possible with a sloppy lawyer, but not with a tough, highly efficient counsel.

In addition to these straightforward methods of research, I might also pick up the telephone and consult with a leading expert in a field. I am never embarrassed to ask for advice. This advice tells me if my judgment is correct. If I get the feeling that I'm on the right track, I then follow it up using other resources.

SOURCES
Part Two

Using Libraries
in Canada
Chapter Fourteen

There are at least three things you can be sure of about libraries: They collect information on *every* subject; the information can *always* be located; and the librarians who run them have been *trained* to meet your information needs.

Surprisingly, libraries are often overlooked as a source of information. This is an irony of monumental proportions, because they are in fact the best source of all. There are thousands of highly skilled librarians across Canada willing to assist anyone involved in research—free of charge—and millions of books, periodicals, specialized collections, and computer services at your fingertips. The only prerequisite for using a library successfully is the ability to ask questions.

There are four types of libraries in Canada: public libraries, academic libraries (on college and university campuses), school libraries, and special libraries (which meet the internal needs of government departments, businesses, and institutions).

Public libraries are tax-supported and are accessible to the public. The policies of academic and school libraries vary, and access can generally be obtained by legitimate researchers. Special libraries, generally speaking, are privately supported and are not always open to the public, although special arrangements can sometimes be made. Let's examine each type of library in greater detail.

Public
Libraries

There are over 3,000 public libraries scattered from coast to coast. Public libraries are governed by provincial laws and regulations and are designed to meet the information needs of local communities. As a resident of a community, you can borrow library materials once you have registered with your nearest library; most libraries issue identification cards that allow the holders to borrow library materials. If you want only to use the facilities, there is no registration requirement, although you should introduce yourself at the reference desk out of politeness.

Dealing with Librarians   Not everyone who works in a library is a librarian. In some smaller libraries, and even in some of the larger ones, professional librarians (who usually have post-graduate training) represent a *minority* of the staff. This is extremely important to realize, because if you can't get the information you need from one member of the library staff, it may be that you're dealing, not with a librarian, but with a community college-educated library technician or a high school graduate with absolutely no training in librarianship. These personnel may very well be able to assist you, but if they can't, don't leave it at that. Ask to speak to a librarian.

Research is very much a social skill, and this is especially evident in a library. You have a right to any information in a public library, but you may walk away empty-handed if you have not handled the staff in a socially acceptable fashion. If you find yourself lining up at an information desk, be patient—it's usually well worth the wait. Avoid wording your request in a negative way or pointing out to the staff that you're unhappy about having to wait. As Gary Goodman says, a pleasant tone of voice yields positive results!

If your research needs are serious, make sure the librarian knows it. Librarians usually point out *basic* sources for everyday, casual information requests. They will spend more time and point out sophisticated sources once they realize that your information request is a serious one.

Vertical Files   An easy way to find information is to use the material in a library's vertical file. A business magazine once asked me to write profiles of 12 Canadian business leaders. I was given only two weeks to complete the job, which left me very little time for the research. I knew almost nothing about the people I was about to interview, but fortunately, the Metropolitan Toronto Library came to my rescue. The person at the information desk told me that the reference library used two filing cabinets to store newspaper and magazine clippings on notable Canadians. Using these files I was able to acquire a quick overview of the business leaders and formulate specific interview questions.

Each library, of course, has its own filing system, and the quality of the material varies considerably from library to library. Larger libraries, which are divided into different subject departments, may or may not use filing cabinets to file material. Inquire at the information desk of each department to find out if such files exist.

Finding Books Quickly   Never walk into a library expecting *all* of its holdings to be listed in one catalogue. Every library has its own way of cataloguing its book collection. There was a time when you could safely assume that all libraries kept a card catalogue to list their books, but with changing technology there are now at least two other popular methods of doing this: various microforms (microfilm and microfiche) and on-line computer services. Most of the smaller libraries still prefer to use card catalogues; more and more of the larger libraries are switching to other space- and cost-saving methods; some libraries use a combination of card catalogues and other methods. The quickest way to sort out this confusion is to ask a reference librarian how the library lists its holdings.

Now you know where to search for a book. If you have to use a microfiche reader (or other equipment for reading microforms) to do this, but you don't know how, don't panic. Most library staff can show you how to use the equipment.

There are different ways to search for books. You can search for the author, title, or subject. Library book catalogues use various combinations of these, all of which are in alphabetical order. It is very common to find the author and title in one catalogue and the subject listings in another.

You may find it difficult at times to identify an author. There isn't any confusion with an author with a name like Jan Grolman, but if the author's name is The Royal Commission on Asbestos, it becomes a little harder. Some libraries divide their authors into personal authors and corporate authors, thus making your job easier, but many libraries don't make this distinction. Ask a reference librarian right from the start how the book catalogue works in that library.

Once you locate the correct title and author of a book, you have to determine where in the library the book is kept. This is more important in smaller- to medium-sized libraries, where you find *open stacks* and select the material yourself. Larger libraries, however, often have *closed stacks*, which means you fill out a book request slip, writing in the call number from the catalogue, hand the slip in at the information desk, and wait for the library staff to bring you the book.

Libraries usually use either the Dewey Decimal System or the Library of Congress System to classify and shelve their books. Public libraries, as a rule, use the Dewey Decimal System, and larger libraries usually use the Library of Congress System. To distinguish between the two, simply look in the upper left-hand corner of the catalogue entry. If the call number is made up of numbers from zero to nine, the library uses the Dewey Decimal System. If the call number contains letters and numbers, the library uses the Library of Congress System (unless you're in a medical library).

Serials   Newspapers, magazines, and journals (which librarians call *serials*) are often catalogued separately from the main library catalogue. The same is generally true of government publications. Again, it is useful to ask the reference librarian how these are indexed.

Interlibrary Loans   If your local library doesn't have a copy of a book or other material you seek, it may be possible to get it through an interlibrary loan. The beauty of Canada's library system is that virtually *all* libraries, regardless of their size, are linked with each other through formal or informal networks. Brian Land pointed this out in Chapter 11. In some provinces libraries are part of a regional system, such as in Nova Scotia, where the provincial library has a catalogue listing the collections of libraries in 11 regions. In this way any library can contact the provincial library, learn which books are kept at which branches, and then arrange an interlibrary loan.

Your last resort when trying to trace a book is to contact the National Library of Canada in Ottawa. This library has a massive card catalogue ("union" catalogue) listing 13 million books in the social sciences and humanities that are available in 300 Canadian libraries. The card catalogue listing ended in 1980; later entries are kept on a computer listing. (Similar union listings of social science and science periodicals are kept at the Canada Institute for Scientific and Technical Information or CISTI. CISTI is in effect the National Science Library.)

The National Library prefers requests to come from a librarian, although it does answer questions directly from the public. With its cataloguing system it can often tell you which libraries keep the books you're looking for. You can then arrange an interlibrary loan through your local library. If you want to locate a Canadian book, the National Library is an excellent source, because part of its mandate is to keep a copy of every book published in Canada. So it can also provide you with information on Canadian subjects, in answer to specific questions, if your local library is unable to help.

The National Library also maintains contact with other libraries around the world. Its collection includes union catalogues from other countries, and it can therefore conduct international literature searches upon request.

Reference Books   All libraries keep a wide selection of reference books, and considerable information can be found by glancing at the right one. Indeed, books have been written on the value of reference books. The comments made here should be taken as an introduction to the topic, nothing more.

To get an idea of the tremendous variety of Canadian reference books, refer to an excellent library science text by Dorothy Ryder, *Canadian Reference Sources*, published by the Canadian Library Association in 1981. Its information is brought up-to-date by an informative article by Edith T. Jarvi and Diane Henderson, "Canadian Reference Books; Or Benevolent Ignorance Dispelled" in a 1983 issue of *Reference Services Review*.

Here are some examples of the variety of reference books available:

I required some information quickly on a Nazi war criminal and found that the history department of my local library had a copy of *Who Was Who in Nazi Germany* by Robert Wistrich. This work answered my questions.

When a friend asked me for information on raising dogs in Canada, the *Directory of Associations in Canada* was very helpful. Figure 14.1 shows a page out of the "Subject Index" of the directory. Under the heading "Dogs" are two references to dog associations, one of which turned out to have all the information I needed. The address of the Canadian Kennel Club appears in Figure 14.2 in the "Alphabetical List of Associations." The directory is really very simple to use.

Whenever I need quick information on Canadian public and

TABLE 14.1   From the *Directory of Associations in Canada*

Subject Index

Dentistry *(continued)*

Newfoundland Dental Hygienists' Association
Nova Scotia Dental Association
Nova Scotia Dental Hygienists Association
Ontario Dental Association
The Ontario Dental Hygienists' Association
Ordre des dentistes du Quebec
Prince Edward Island Dental Hygienists' Association
Provincial Dental Board of Nova Scotia
The Royal College of Dental Surgeons of Canada
The Royal College of Dental Surgeons of Ontario
The Royal College of Dentists of Canada
Saskatchewan Dental Hygienists' Association
Western Canada Dental Society
Western Commercial Dental Laboratories Labour Relations Association

Dermatologie *Voir* **Dermatology**

Dermatology
Canadian Dermatological Association

Design, Book *See* **Book Trade**

Design, Industrial *See* **Industrial Design**

Design, Interior *See* **Interior Design**

Dessin Technique *Voir* **Industrial Design**

Detaillants *Voir* **Retail Trade**

Detergents *See* **Soaps and Detergents**

Detersifs *Voir* **Soaps and Detergents**

Distributeurs automatiques *Voir* **Vending Machines**

Distributeurs d'automobiles *Voir* **Automobile Dealers**

Distribution (Commerce) *Voir* **Marketing**

Diving
Alberta Scuba Divers Council
Aquatic Hall of Fame and Museum of Canada Inc.
Association of Canadian Underwater Councils
Canadian Amateur Diving Association
Federation quebecoise de plongeon amateur inc.
Federation quebecoise des activites subaquatiques
Manitoba Underwater Council
New Brunswick Underwater Council
Newfoundland and Labrador Underwater Federation
Northwest Territories Underwater Council
Nova Scotia Underwater Council
Ontario Underwater Council
Prince Edward Island Underwater Council
Saskatchewan Underwater Council
The Underwater Club of Canada Incorporated
Yukon Underwater Divers Association

Doctors *See* **Physicians' and Surgeons' Associations**

Documents Officiels, Organisation de *Voir* **Records Management**

See Also Alcoholism
Alcohol & Drug Concerns, Inc.
Alcohol and Drug Dependency Information and Counselling Services
Alcoholism and Drug Addiction Research Foundation
Canadian Addictions Foundation
Council on Drug Abuse

Drugs *See* **Alcoholism**

Drugs *See* **Drug Addiction**

Drugs *See* **Pharmacy**

Drugs *See* **Temperance**

Drywall Construction
Pacific Drywall Dealers Association

Dutch *See* **Netherlanders**

Dystrophie Musculaire *Voir* **Muscular Dystrophy**

Earth Sciences *See* **Geology**

Eau *Voir* **Water and Water Works**

Eau, Pollution de l' *Voir* **Pollution**

Eaus d'Egouts *Voir* **Sanitation and Sewer Construction**

Ebenisterie *Voir* **Woodworking**

Echecs *Voir* **Chess**

Developpement Economique et Industriel *Voir* **Economic and Industrial Development**

Developpement Industriel *Voir* **Economic and Industrial Development**

Developpement Urbain *Voir* **Urban Development**

Diabete *Voir* **Diabetes**

Diabetes
Association du diabète du Québec inc.
Canadian Diabetes Association
Juvenile Diabetes Research Foundation

Diamond Drilling *See* **Drilling and Boring**

Die Casting
See Also Foundry Industry; Tools
Canadian Die Casters Association

Dietetics *See* **Nutrition**

Dietetiques *Voir* **Nutrition**

Dimanche *Voir* **Sabbath**

Dindes *Voir* **Poultry**

Direct Mail *See* **Advertising**

Dirigeants *Voir* **Executives Associations**

Disabled *See* **Handicapped**

Disques *Voir* **Records and Recording**

Distilleries *Voir* **Liquor**

Distilling *See* **Liquor**

Dogs
Canadian Kennel Club
The National Retriever Club of Canada

Dolphins
The Whale Society of Edmonton

Doors *See* **Building Materials and Supplies**

Dossiers Médicaux *Voir* **Medical Records**

Drama *See* **Authorship**

Drama *See* **Performing Arts**

Dresses *See* **Clothing**

Drilling and Boring
Canadian Association of Drilling Engineers
Canadian Association of Oilwell Drilling Contractors
Canadian Diamond Drilling Association
Canadian Drilling Research Association

Driver Education
Young Drivers of Canada

Droit *Voir* **Law**

Droit d'Auteur *Voir* **Copyright, Patents and Trademarks**

Droit de Propriété *Voir* **Real Estate**

Droit de Publication *Voir* **Copyright, Patents and Trademarks**

Droit de Reproduction *Voir* **Copyright, Patents and Trademarks**

Droits Civiques *Voir* **Civil Liberties**

Drug Addiction

Eclairage *Voir* **Illumination Engineering**

Ecoles *Voir* **Schools**

Ecologie *Voir* **Conservation and the Environment**

Ecology *See* **Conservation and the Environment**

Economic and Industrial Development
See Also Business; Chambers of Commerce; Manufacturing; Tourist Trade; Urban Development
Atlantic Provinces Economic Council
Great Lakes Waterways Development Association
Industrial Developers Association of Canada
Ontario Industrial Development Council, Incorporated
Organisation catholique canadienne pour le developpement et la paix

Economic and Social Assistance (Domestic)
See Also Anti-Poverty Organizations; Citizenship and Immigration; Clubs and Service Clubs; Counselling and Guidance; Criminology and Corrections; Economic and Social Assistance (International); Fraternal Organizations; Social Planning Councils; Social Work; Veterans' Associations; Volunteer Services; Youth; Philanthropy
Allied Jewish Community Services of Montreal
Association des administrateurs des finances des services de santé et des services sociaux du Québec
Association des administrateurs des services administratifs des services de santé et des services sociaux du Québec

TABLE 14.2   From the *Directory of Associations in Canada*

Alphabetical List of Associations/Liste alphabétique des associations

Canadian International DX Radio Club (1962)
169 Grandview Ave., Winnipeg, Man.   R2G 0L4
(204) 339-2983
Exec. Sec.: R.L. Jennings
Mem.: 1000
Pub.: Monthly

**Canadian International Freight Forwarders Association Inc./
Association des transitaires internationaux canadiens inc.**
(1948)
P.O. Box 156, Place d'Armes, Montreal, Que.
H2Y 3E9
(514) 697-2111
Sec. Mgr.: George A. Sloan
Emp.: 2   *Mem.:* 150
Pub.: Newsletter, monthly
▲ 1981, Toronto, Ont.; 1982, Montreal, Que.; 1983,
Vancouver, B.C.

**Canadian Interuniversity Athletic Union/Union sportive
interuniversitaire canadienne** (1961)
333 River Rd., Suite 1117, Vanier, Ont.   K1L
8B9
(613) 744-2573
Exec. Vice-Pres.: Robert W. Pugh
Pub.: newsletters, monthly
▲ June 15-18, 1981 Ottawa, Ont.
Formed by merger of/Par amalgam de: Canadian
Women's Intercollegiate Athletic Union, Canadian
Intercollegiate Athletic Union

The Canadian Intravenous Nurses Association
4433 Sheppard Ave. East, Suite 200, Agincourt,
Ont.   M1S 1V3

Canadian Islamic Cultural and Educational Foundation
9014-90th St., Edmonton, Alta.   T6C 3L9

Canadian Jewellers Institute (1945)
100 Front St. West, Toronto, Ont.   M5J 1E3
(416) 368-8372
Exec. Dir.: Donald Klinger
Emp.: 6   *Mem.:* 1,500
Pub.: Canadian Jewellers Institute Newsviews, q
▲ 1981, May, Victoria, B.C.; 1982, May, Ottawa,
Ont.; 1983, May, Pointe-au-Pic, Que.

Canadian Jewish Congress/Congrès juif canadien
1590 Ave Dr. Penfield, Montreal, Que.

- **Ontario Region** (1919)
150 Beverley St., Toronto, Ont.   M5T 1Y6
(416) 977-3811
Exec. Dir.:

**Canadian Jiu-jitsu Association/Association canadienne de
jiu-jitsu**
Vice-Pres.: Hal Batke
74 Captain Rolph Ct., Markham, Ont.   L3P 3K9

Canadian Job Therapy Association *See* **M2/W2 Association
- Christian Volunteers in Corrections**

Canadian Judicial Council
130 Albert St., Suite 1705, Ottawa, Ont.   K1P
5G4

Canadian Karting Federation
C/O P.O. Box 65, Stn. A, Weston, Ont.   M9N 3M6
(416) 626-1934

**Canadian Kendo Federation/Fédération canadienne de
Kendo**
Pres.: Misaho Noda
8349 Elliott St., Vancouver, B.C.   V5S 2P3

- **Quebec Region/Région de Quebec**
2112, rue Frontenac, 2e etage, Montreal, Que.
H2K 2Z3
Dir. reg.: Jean-Jacques Jauniaux

Canadian Lacombe (Swine) Breeders Assoc. (1958)
Box 122, Breton, Alta.   T0G 0P0
(403) 696-2458
Sec.: George Croome
Emp.: 1   *Mem.:* 85
Pub.: Newsletter, quarterly
▲ 1981, March, Winnipeg, Man.

Canadian Lacrosse Hall of Fame
1807 Hamilton St., New Westminster, B.C.   V3M
2P3
Armstrong: W.R. Armstron

**Canadian Ladies Curling Association/L'Association
canadienne féminine de curling** (1960)
Pres.: Caroline M. Ball
P.O. Box 187, Grand Falls, Nfld.   A2A 2J7
(709) 489-2230
Emp.: 2   *Mem.:* 70,000
Pub.: Newsletter, quarterly
▲ 1981, Nfld.; 1982, Sask.; 1983, B.C.

**Canadian Ladies' Golf Association/Association canadienne
des golfeuses** (1913)
333 River Rd., Ottawa, Ont.   K1L 8B9
(613) 746-5564
Exec. Dir.: Les Whamond
Emp.: 2   *Mem.:* 63,000
Pub.: CLGA Year Book
▲ 1981, Nov. 28, Charlottetown, P.E.I.; 1982, Nov.
27, Vancouver, B.C.; 1983, Nov. 26, Edmonton,
Alta.

Canadian Italian Business and Professional Association of Toronto/L'Association des hommes d'affaires et professionnels canadiens-italiens (1951)
750 Oakdale Rd., Suite 54, Downsview, Ont.
M3N 2L4
(416) 743-7730
Gen. Mgr.: Robert Dante Martella
Emp.: 2   *Mem.:* 440
Pub.: Bi-monthly journal, annual directory
▲ 1981, 1982, 1983: Sept., Toronto, Ont.

Canadian-Italian Business & Professional Men's Association of Quebec Inc. *See/Voir* **L'Association des hommes d'affaires & professionnels canadiens-italiens du Quebec inc.**

Canadian Jersey Cattle Club (1901)   N1H 3K1
343 Waterloo Ave., Guelph, Ont.
(519) 821-1020
Sec. Mgr.: Cameron Honderich
Emp.: 6   *Mem.:* 690
Pub.: Canadian Jersey Breeder, m.
▲ 1981. Calgary, Alta.

Canadian Jesuit Missions (1955)
833 Broadview Ave., Toronto, Ont.   M4K 2P9
(416) 466-1195
Pres.: E. Peter W. Nash
Emp.: 4
Pub.: Canadian Jesuit Missions, bi-m.
▲ 1981, 1982, 1983: Nov., Toronto, Ont.

Canadian Jewellers Association (1918)
100 Front St. West, Toronto, Ont.   M5J 1E3
(416) 368-8372
Exec. Dir.: Donald Klinger
Emp.: 7   *Mem.:* 795
Pub.: Canadian Jewellery News, q.
▲ 1981. May, Victoria, B.C.; 1982. May, Ottawa, Ont.; 1983. May, Point au Pic, Que.

Canadian Kennel Club/Le Cercle canadien du chenil (1888)
2150 Bloor St. West, Toronto, Ont.   M6S 4V7
(416) 763-4391
Sec. Treas.: John C. Gough
Emp.: 70   *Mem.:* 12,200
Pub.: Monthly
▲ 1981. March, P.E.I.

Canadian Kitchen Cabinet Association/Association canadienne des cabinets de cuisine (1969)
80 Flaming Roseway, Willowdale, Ont.   M2N 5W8
(416) 226-0642
Exec. Vice Pres.: Peter E. Woodger
Emp.: 1   *Mem.:* 95
▲ 1981. Quebec, Que.; 1982. Victoria, B.C.; 1983. Jasper, Alta.

Canadian Labour Congress/Congrès du travail du Canada
2841 Riverside Dr., Ottawa, Ont.   K1V 8X7
(613) 521-3400
Pres.: Dennis McDermott
Emp.: 118   *Mem.:* 2,329,067 in 202 unions
Pub.: Canadian Labour/Travailleur canadian, bi-w.
▲ Biennial. 1982

- Atlantic Region
96 Norwood Ave., Suite 208, Moncton, N.B.   E1C 6L9
Reg. Dir.: Allister MacLeod

- Ontario Region
15 Gervais Dr., Suite 206, Don Nills, Ont.   M3C 1Y8
Reg. Dir.: Ralph Ortlieb

- Pacific Region
4925 Canada Way, Suite 213, Burnaby, B.C.   V5G 1M1
Reg. Dir.: W.V. Smalley

- Prairie Region
2709 12th Ave., Suite 107, Regna, Sask.   S4T 1J3
Reg. Dir.: E.W. Northeim

- Alberta Branch
Rep.: Frances Peace
42 Rosery Dr. N.W., Calgary, Alta.   T2K 1L7

Canadian Ladies Lawn Bowling Council (1972)
Sec.: Mrs. Molly Knox
40 Old Surrey Lane, Victoria Place, Bobcaygeon, R.R. 31, Ont.   K0M 1A0
Mem.: 7,000
Pub.: The Green, q.
▲ 1981. Aug., Vancouver, B.C.; 1982. Aug., Winnipeg, Man.; 1983. Aug., Calgary, Alta.

Canadian Lamp and Fixture Manufacturers Association Inc./Association canadienne des fabricants de lampes et luminaires inc.
90 Rue Savard, Auteuil, Que.   H7H 1M7
(514) 625-0096

Canadian Land and Reclamation Association (1975)
P.O. Box 682, Guelph, Ont.   N1H 6L3
Sec.: Dr. J.E. Winch
Emp.: 1   *Mem.:* 300
Pub.: Reclamation Review, q.: *Reclamation Newsletter*, s.a.
▲ 1981. Kimberley, B.C.; 1982. Sydney, N.S.

Canadian Landrace Swine Breeders Association
Stroud, Ont.   L0L 2M0
Sec. Mgr.: Wm. T. New

Canadian Latvian Business and Professional Association (1954)
Pres.: Alexsander Budrevics
123 Overland Dr., Don Mills, Ont.   M3G 2C7
(416) 444-5201
Mem.: 150
Pub.: Quarterly newsletter in Latvian
▲ 1981, 1982, 1983 Toronto, Ont.

private companies, I begin by referring to Brian Land's classic reference book, *Sources of Information for Canadian Business*, published by the Canadian Chamber of Commerce.

You can be assured that whatever your subject, there is a handy reference book on it.

Indexes   If you want to locate an article in a newspaper, magazine, journal, or report, you should familiarize yourself with indexes. These are usually thick books that appear intimidating because of their size, small print, and numerous abbreviated forms. With a little practice, however, you will find that indexes are not complicated to use and in fact can save you the tedious job of skimming through countless back issues of periodicals. In Canada there are at least four key indexes you should be aware of.

The *Canadian News Index* (CNI), published by Micromedia Limited, Toronto, indexes seven of the country's major daily newspapers: the *Calgary Herald*, the *Toronto Star*, the *Globe and Mail*, the *Vancouver Sun*, the *Winnipeg Free Press*, the *Montreal Gazette*, and the *Halifax Chronicle Herald*.

CNI is published monthly in a magazine format, and the issues are republished in one volume at the end of each year. It is separated into two sections; the bulk of the references comprise the "Subject Index." If, for example, you want to know what articles have been written on the asbestos industry in Canada, look under the subject heading "Asbestos Industry." In Figure 14.3, part-way down the right-hand column, there is a reference to a feature article that appeared in the *Globe and Mail* on January 6, 1982.

Figure 14.4 shows the key to abbreviations used in the CNI. The letter "F" in square brackets indicates a feature article. You can easily distinguish between features [F], letters to the editor [L], and editorials [Ed]. This, along with the title of the article, can help narrow down your search.

If you are researching an individual, for example, Canadian nationalist Mel Hurtig, you would look under the "Biographical Index." Under his name, in the lower half of Figure 14.3, two articles are listed. If you are interested only in feature articles, you can limit yourself to references marked [F].

Micromedia also publishes the *Canadian Business Index* (CBI), which indexes 164 leading Canadian business magazines. Like the CNI, it is published monthly and as a single-volume index at the end of each year. Three distinct sections of the CBI enable a researcher to

TABLE 14.3   From the *Canadian News Index*

SUBJECT INDEX

Apartment buildings (cont'd.)
Grand style thrives in old Montreal apartments [F] * *MG* Ja 4'82 p19
Building loans 'to spark starts' *VS* Ja 7'82 pC7
Luxury apartment units 'typical' of BC Lower Mainland *VS* Ja 13'82 pB1

Appliances
See Household appliances

Appraisal
See Real property — Valuation

Aquatics
1.200 chilly polar bear swimmers take frigid dip in bay *VS* Ja 2'82 pA3
Canadian Davis swims to world-best mark *MG* Ja 11'82 p15
Davis' swim record now reality at US International *VS* Ja 11'82 pB4
Hospital to get underwater help; Meek to swim Lake Ontario for Sick Kids *G & M* Ja 12'82 p4

Aquitaine Co of Canada Ltd
CDC concludes Aquitaine deal *CH* Ja 7'82 pC1

Arab countries
Arab world urged to back Saudi plan, 'put Israel on spot' *G & M* Ja 4'82 p10

Archaeology
Archeologist fears looters may find Brule's grave first *G & M* Ja 4'82 p1

Architecture
See also Buildings
Architect Gaboury enjoys link with past [F] * *WFP* Ja 5'82 p17
Architect for Elmwood Club, Ostiguy is accused of incompetence *G & M* Ja 7'82 p5
The tri-colored flag of architecture: restoration, preservation and conservation *G & M* Ja 7'82 pE3
Architect Bent in fix for convention centre remarks *G & M* Ja 8'82 p3
Early success for a young architect* *HCH* Ja 11'82 p22
The architect's hearing as Bent criticizes Toronto Convention Centre [Ed] *G & M* Ja 14'82 p6
Architects sketch Views of what their job's about [F] * *MG* Ja 16'82 p37
Critic of convention centre Colin Bent is muzzled—Sewell *G & M* Ja 23'82 pE19

Art (cont'd.)
In years since Holocaust; Gershon Iskowitz has moved from death-camp memories to abstract works based on the landscape of his adopted country [F] * *TS* Ja 23'82 pF5
McMichael fuss entering Round 2 *G & M* Ja 26'82 p4
Art and science merge in Jack Butler's studio* *WFP* Ja 30'82 p31
Artist Phil Richards has a penchant for patterns, historical works in his art [F] * *TS* Ja 30'82 pH5

Art galleries
See Museums and galleries

Artificial insemination
Artificial insemination: 2,000 Montreal children have been born through this simple process since 1971 [F] *MG* Ja 9'82 p37

Asbestos industry
Asbestos slump is expected to stay until 2nd quarter [F] *G & M* Ja 6'82 pB1

Assault
See Crime and criminals — Assault

Astronautics
See also Communications satellites
Russians, Japanese search for life in space [F] *G & M* Ja 4'82 p9
A down-to-Earth look at factories in outer space [F] *G & M* Ja 25'82 p9

Astronomy
Cosmic rethink: Does universe have a cellular structure—Nobel scientist Alfven [F] * *CH* Ja 16'82 pH17
Halley's Comet: quarry of the century [F] * *CH* Ja 2'82 pC5
Star gazing could be a thing of the past *CH* Ja 9'82 pJ21
Calgary eyed as centre for $30-million radio-telescope system stretching across Canada *CH* Ja 28'82 pB5
University of Calgary astrophysicists make others' notice [F] * *CH* Ja 30'82 pF9

Athletics
See Sports and athletics

BIOGRAPHICAL INDEX

Gray, Herb
Gray emerges as a survivor *CH* Ja 14'82 pA10
Gray, Jim
Alberta crusader a perpetual doer *CH* Ja 25'82 pB5
Greene-Raine, Nancy
Canada's snowbird remains unchanged [F] * *CH* Ja 16'82 pH2
Gretzky, Wayne
Escape from stardom: Gretzky's toughest job [F] *G & M* Ja 15'82 p37
50 goals great, now Edmonton awaits next miracle by Gretzky [F] *G & M* Ja 1'82 p29
The Gretzky deal: $20 million in 15 years *G & M* Ja 21'82 p1
Gretzkynomics: Supply and demand being answered—McGillivray [C] * *CH* Ja 27'82 pB2
Wayne Gretzky: Portrait of the artist as a young man [F] * *MG* Ja 2'82 p21
Wayne's Place was in the spotlight* *CH* Ja 16'82 pA12
Hackworth, Donald
Troubled times give GM Canada's new boss his most serious test [F] * *MG* Ja 30'82 p63
Haig, Alexander
The world according to Haig: Interview [F] ** *TS* Ja 19'82 pA10
Haig: 'Greatest revival since Lazarus'* *VS* Ja 11'82 pA12
Haig revival reminiscent of Lazarus [F] * *WFP* Ja 13'82 p10
Haig's revival seen as greatest resurrection act since Lazarus—analysis* *SS* Ja 10'82 pB2

Hitschmanova, Lotta
Hitschmanova quits top post of relief agency *MG* Ja 2'82 p6
Hoard, 'Mad Mike'
Seychelles: Colonel Mad Mike's Last Hurrah. How two gross blunders foiled the most infamous of Africa's 'dogs of war' [F] * # *TS* Ja 2'82 pB6
Hoebig, Desmond
Hoebig and Tunis largely unknown, but nudging their way to the top in cello and piano* *HCH* Ja 27'82 p2E
Holloway, Stanley
Actor dies at 91 *VS* Ja 30'82 pA1
Actor Stan Holloway on stage for 70 years* *VS* Ja 30'82 pH1
Horikoshi, Jiro
Designer of wartime Japan's famed Zero fighter dies in Tokyo *WFP* Ja 12'82 p42
Howe, Foster (Bud)
32-year RCMP veteran appointed commanding officer for Metro *TS* Ja 6'82 pA12
Howland, William
The informal William Howland [F] * *G & M* Ja 30'82 p18
Humphrey, John Nelson, Dr
Obituary *TS* Ja 23'82 pA15
Hurtig, Mel
Here comes Hurtig's mega-project* *CH* Ja 30'82 pF6
Mel Hurtig says he does not hate the US [C] *WFP* Ja 5'82 p7
Irish, Edward Simmons (Ned)
Obituary *WFP* Ja 22'82 p53
Iskowitz, Gershon
In years since Holocaust; Gershon Iskowitz has moved from death-

Kirby, Cecil (cont'd.)
Killer Kirby given 2nd deal for immunity, money [F] *G & M* Ja 28'82 p1
Lawyer Caroline says Kirby needed as witness hidden by Ontario police *G & M* Ja 26'82 p1
Pact to protect Kirby upheld by Kaplan *G & M* Ja 29'82 p1
Second deal with Kirby necessary to clarify the first—McMurtry *G & M* Ja 29'82 p4
Stories on Kirby in Globe don't serve justice—McMurtry *G & M* Ja 30'82 p1
Kirby, Michael
Kirby doesn't consider new job a demotion *HCH* Ja 9'82 p2
Kirby not the fishery's chequebook savior [F] * *G & M* Ja 19'82 p8
Michael JL Kirby, PhD, is going into fish—Valpy [C] *G & M* Ja 21'82 p6
Michael Kirby: Civil servant on the move* *SS* Ja 10'82 pA6
Why is Kirby going to Fisheries?—Harris [C] *G & M* Ja 21'82 p8
Kitto, HDF
Obituary *MG* Ja 26'82 p48
Obituary *TS* Ja 26'82 pA18
Klein, Ralph
Calgary goes into a de-Klein [Ed] *CH* Ja 9'82 pA6
It's a bum rap for Klein *CH* Ja 29'82 pB1
Klein admits city's image hurt by speech *CH* Ja 20'82 pB1
Klein's letter may not fix damage—Bell *CH* Ja 12'82 pB1
'Mr Communicator' loses his cool—and his touch—Anderson [C] *CH* Ja 9'82 pB1

TABLE 14.4   From the *Canadian News Index*

Abbreviations

&	And	D	December	m	million	Sask	Saskatchewan
Ag	August	Dept	Department	Man	Manitoba	Soc	Society
Alta	Alberta	Edmn	Edmonton	Metro	Metropolitan	Spr	Spring
Ap	April	F	February	Mfr	Manufacturer	Summ	Summer
Asrn	Assurance	Grp	Group	Mr	March	Tor	Toronto
Assn	Association	Hal	Halifax	Mtl	Montreal	Van	Vancouver
Assocs	Associates	Inc	Incorporated	My	May	Whlr	Wholesaler
b	Billion		Incorporation	N	November	Wpg	Winnipeg
BC	British Columbia	Ins	Insert	NB	New Brunswick	Wint	Winter
Bd	Board	Inst	Institute, Institutional	NS	Nova Scotia	YT	Yukon Territory
Bros	Brothers	Insur	Insurance	NWT	Northwest Territories	#	Tabular or graphic illustration accompanies article
Cal	Calgary	Intl	International	Natl	National		
Cmsn	Commission	Ja	January	Nfld	Newfoundland	*	Photograph accompanies article
Cmte	Committee	Je	June	O	October		
Cndn	Canadian	Jl	July	Ont	Ontario	[C]	Regular column
Co(s)	Company(ies)	Jr	Junior	Org	Organization	[F]	Feature article
Coop	Co-operative	Lab	Laboratory	PEI	Prince Edward Island	[Ed]	Editorial
Corp	Corporation.	Ltd	Limited	Que	Quebec	[L]	Letter to the editor
Corp	Corporate	Ltee	Limitee	S	September	•	Noteworthy article

search for articles by subject, corporate name, and personal name—
or cross-reference all three. A sample of this reference tool is
reproduced in Figure 14.5.

TABLE 14.5   From the *Canadian Business Index*

SUBJECT INDEX

Automobiles (contd.)
Automakers report November sales gains *Fin T*
70[28]D 7'81 p14
FADA members gloomy about 82's prospects* *G*
& M D 12'81 pB20
Diesel car sales climb as gas prices rise *G & M D*
30'81 pB13
Automobiles, Company-owned
Company cars will be less popular* *Fin T* 70[30]D
21'81 p15
Users of co autos face paper war, tax experts warn
G & M D 22'81 p5
Automobiles, Electric
See Electric vehicles
Automobiles, Foreign
Import limits hit Subaru* *Fin P West* D 5'81
pW1-2
.Export curbs put brakes on Japanese auto prod* *G*
& M D 14'81 pB26
Sales
Nov car imports up 5.3% *G & M D* 12'81 pB8
Automotive industry
Total payout set at $.85 on $1 at White Cda *G &
M D* 16'81 pB1
See also Automobile industry;
Motor truck industry
Imports and exports
See Automobiles — Imports and exports

Banks and banking (contd.)
Who's stuck if cheque bounces? Surprise—it could
be bank *G & M D* 22'81 p1-2
See also Banks and banking, Central; Cheques;
Electronic data processing [applications] —
Banks and banking; Foreign exchange; Interest;
Transfer of funds; Trust companies
See also "Banking is News" in issues of Canadian
Banker & ICB Review
Accounting
See Bank accounting
Corporate services
Managing your bank relationship *Bus Quart*
46[4]D'81 p39-46
Credit service
Farmers, bankers and credit* *Can Bank* 88[6]D'81
p68
Banks clamp down on firms' elbow room *Fin P*
75[44]D 5'81 p30
Banks move closer to farmers *Fin P West* D 26'81
pW7
See also Bank credit cards
Electronic data processing
See Electronic data processing [applications] —
Banks and banking
Finance
Royal Bank raises profit *G & M D* 2'81 pB9
Bank profits may be mixed blessings # *G & M D*
5'81 pB20

CORPORATE NAME INDEX

Hydro-Quebec (contd.)
Spending plans for '82 receive 7% trim *Energy
Ana* 10[49]D 18'81 p4

I

Imasco Limited**
Floats 7-yr note issue *G & M D* 2'81 pB22
Imasco unit to buy Burger Chef for $44m (US) *G
& M D* 10'81 pB6
Imasco buys into bigger US league *Fin P* 75[50]D
19'81 p22
Imperial Oil Limited**
New chairman *Fin T* 70[28]D 7'81 p28
Price low, timing bad for buying Imperial Oil
shares # *G & M D* 14'81 pB8
Securities analysis: best suited to survive # *Fin T*
70[29]D 14'81 p24
Imperial plans oil sands talks *G & M D* 19'81 pB3
Securities recommendation—buy *Inv Digest*
13[24]D 22'81 p374
Inco Metals Co
Weak demand for nickel forces cutbacks *G & M D*
5'81 pB3
Inglis Limited**
Inglis has inside track but Admiral may get other
bids *G & M D* 12'81 pB3

Interprovincial Pipe Line Limited**
Securities recommendation—buy *Inv Rep* 41[43]D
4'81 p341
Marks 25 years of growth* *Oilwk* 32[46]D 21'81
p12-14 +
Inverness Petroleum Ltd.**
Takes new direction *Oilwk* 32[44]D 7'81 p91-92
Co study/securities analysis *Inv Digest* 13[24]D
22'81 p382
Investment Dealers' Assn of Can
Brief *Bus Life* 9[12]D'81 p11
Irwin-Dorsey Ltd**
Shuts down *Q & Quire* 47[12]D'81 p16
Irwin Toy Limited**
Sets up licensing division *Vol Ret* 33[12]D'81 p2
[Irwin Toy: what a difference a yr makes] *G & M*
D 5'81 pB3
ISO Mines Ltd**
See Teck Corporation
Isuzu Motors Ltd
Co study/securities recommendation = -buy # *Inv
Digest* 13[23]D 8'81 p363
Ivaco Inc.**
Securities recommendation—hold *Inv Rep*
41[44]D 11'81 p354
Securities analysis: overlooked by investors *Fin T*
70[30]D 21'81 p25

PERSONAL NAME INDEX

Peterson, Robert B
Esso Resources appt* *Fin P* 75[49]D
12'81 p25
Esso Resources appt* *Fin P West* D
12'81 pW7
Esso Resources appt* *Fin T* 70[29]D
14'81 p2 .
Esso Resources appt* *Oilwk*
32[46]D 21'81 p39
Pezim, Murray
Galveston Petroleums appt *Oilwk*
32[46]D 21'81 p38
Pielsticker, Charles A
Misener Holdings appt* *G & M D*
11'81 pB13
Pillar, Charles L
International Geosystems Corp appt
* *G & M D* 18'81 pB2
Pinker, Robert
AuthorBR *C Pub Admin*
24[4]Winter'81 p641-648
Poitras, OA
Commercial Credit Corp appt* *G &*

Santos, Humberto
Equipment Lessors Assn appt* *G &
M D* 2'81 pB11
Sastry, Kalanadh VS
Author* *CIM* 74[836]D'81 p43-53
Savage, Al
TTC appt* *Civic* 33[11]N'81 p33-34
Schurman, paul
CJRW community radio* *Broad*
40[12]D'81 p43-44
Scurfield, Ralph T
Interview* *BC Bus* 9[12]D'81 p72-73

Nu-West Grp appt* *Fin P* 75[44]D
5'81 p12
TransAlta Utilities appt* *G & M D*
7'81 pB7
Transalta Utilites appt* *Fin P*
75[49]D 12'81 p26
Nu-West Group appt* *Oilwk*
32[45]D 14'81 p74
TransAlta Utilities appt* *Fin T*
70[29]D 14'81 p3

Thurow, Lester C
AuthorBR *Ind Rel* 36[4]Winter'81
p949-951
Touhy, Carolyn J
Author *C Pub Admin*
24[4]Winter'81 p653-655
Towe, Peter
Petro-Canada Intl appt *Oilwk*
32[44]D 7'81 p97
Traquair, Brian
Author* *Computer* 6[12]D'81
p58,60 +
Trudeau, Pierre
Que gave up own veto: PM *G & M
D* 2'81 p1
Might be 'roped into' staying to fight
separatists: Trudeau *G & M D*
4'81 p1-2
Rates 'your fault, not mine': PM *G
& M D* 4'81 p1
PM rebuffs Levesque over patriation
move *G & M D* 5'81 p1-2
Tucker, Ed

You can use the *Microlog Index* to search for municipal, provincial, and federal government publications, as well as privately published materials from non-government research institutions, professional associations, and special interest groups. The index, also published by Micromedia, is divided into a main section (which lists all materials by individual and corporate authors), subject section, and title section.

One of Canada's oldest indexes is the *Canadian Periodical Index*, edited by the Canadian Library Association. It dates back to at least 1928 and indexes approximately 130 French and English periodicals, many of which are not included in the indexes mentioned above.

Many other publications are not included in these indexes. Some publications, such as the *New York Times*, publish their own. To find out if the publication you seek has a separate index or is indexed in a central source, refer to *Ulrich's International Periodicals Directory* or the *Standard Periodical Directory*.

Computer Services   Indexes are becoming increasingly available on computer services. Many of the larger public libraries now subscribe to on-line services that can perform literature searches. "On-line" simply refers to equipment connected to a computer to extract information, such as the telephone. Sometimes the full text of an article can be produced, but in the majority of cases only the citation of the article appears. Libraries do not charge you for the consulting period while your question is being narrowed down, but you have to pay for computer time.

Most of the major computer services are American-based but offer Canadian material as well. Many of these services began in the late 1960s, which means that a manual search is required to locate earlier material.

Dialog® Information Services Incorporated is one of the more popular on-line services. With over 55 million records in 200 data bases and still rapidly expanding, it is considered the world's largest on-line service. One data base alone combines the *Canadian News Index* and the *Canadian Business Index*. Another data base, "Disclosure II," carries information on some key Canadian companies.

Another competing service, Orbit, offers a similar diversity, with 70 data bases of information—everything from voting records to conference papers. Medlars provides medical information from the U.S. National Library of Medicine. Info Globe offers a list of articles and the full text of stories published in the *Globe and Mail* from November 14, 1977 to the present.

Many other services exist. To discover the tremendous diversity, refer to *Omni Online Database Directory* by Mike Edelhart and Owen Davies, published by Collier Macmillan.

Locating Publications and Libraries   Because most computer searches only list the article and do not reproduce the actual text, a researcher still has to find which libraries carry the publication. Most larger libraries carry a healthy collection of serials, including the publications discussed earlier in this chapter under "Indexes." If your library doesn't subscribe to the publications you seek, locate a library that does and then arrange an interlibrary loan through your local library.

Various directories help you locate the libraries in your area. For an exhaustive list of these directories, consult the helpful booklet, *Directories of Canadian Libraries* by J. Tomlinson. It's available free of charge by writing to the Library Documentation Centre, National Library of Canada, 395 Wellington Street, Ottawa, Ontario, K1A 0N4 or by telephoning (613) 995-8717.

This booklet is helpful if you encounter difficulties. The *Canadian Library Handbook*, which lists 4,300 public and special libraries according to location, subject, and name, is often sufficient, as are *The Source Book: The Corpus Almanac* and the *Canadian Almanac and Directory*. The *American Library Directory* is especially helpful in that it gives the size of a library's collection and its budget; this information can help you determine the likelihood of a library subscribing to the journals you seek.

Another useful directory to keep in mind when searching for libraries is *Subject Collections: A Guide to Special Book Collections*, edited by Lee Ash. These specialized collections may include copies of obscure publications you seek. For example, if you were researching the great English author Sir Arthur Conan Doyle and wanted back copies of *Strand* magazine, where his early Sherlock Holmes stories first appeared, you would find that this directory lists the "Sir Arthur Conan Doyle Collection" in the Metropolitan Toronto Library: That reference library holds back copies of *Strand*.

If you can't arrange an interlibrary loan, you may have to write directly to the publisher for back copies of a publication. If you need an article or report listed in any of the indexes published by Micromedia, you can purchase them directly from Micromedia

Limited, Document Delivery Service, 144 Front Street West, Toronto, Ontario, M5J 2L7.

Using Libraries to Find Experts   One of the fundamental principles of research is to attempt to acquire the information we need from experts who have already done the research. The trick, of course, is to find the right expert, and for this, too, libraries can be useful. Larger libraries are divided into specialized departments, from business to fine art, and each department keeps professional directories. If, for example, you wanted to find a local expert who could interpret financial data, you would find the latest issue of *The Financial Analysts Federation Membership Directory* in the business department of your library. (It is always a good practice to refer to the latest issue of any directory, because the information can become outdated quickly.) Most professional groups, in fact, publish membership directories such as this one.

The general reference department of a library keeps the *Directory of Associations in Canada*, which lists about 10,000 international, national, interprovincial, and provincial organizations in Canada. It also provides the association's name, address, elected officials, and information on annual meetings. Each of these associations has members who are experts. If you call the wrong group, chances are you can be referred to a more suitable organization.

To supplement this directory, you can conduct a newspaper search; newspapers often quote experts and organizations. It can also be fruitful to check with a library's department head. Librarians usually keep abreast of who is doing research in what field.

Finally, you can contact the editors of trade publications directly. Trade editors, such as those at Maclean Hunter and Southam Communications, are often more knowledgeable than librarians about the information sources available in their field.

Finding Freelance Researchers   There may be an occasion when you don't have the time to do your own research, and you may wish to hire a freelance researcher. Local librarians can often refer you to one because librarians, particularly department heads, generally know of the freelance researchers who use their facilities.

There is also a new, handy directory available at many libraries, *Who Knows What: Canadian Library-Related Expertise*, which provides a 174-page list of Canadian librarians and other research experts, including freelance researchers. It was compiled by Susan

Klement for the Canadian Library Association and is expected to be updated at least bi-annually.

In addition, there is the *Directory of Survey Organizations*, published by Statistics Canada, which lists hundreds of organizations providing research services to federal government departments. Unfortunately, the most recent edition was published in 1981, but a revised edition is expected in 1985. Many of the listings in the 1981 edition, however, are still accurate. This is an especially good source if you need to do any type of market research.

A similar, larger directory is *Information Sources*, published annually by the Information Industry Association, 316 Pennsylvania Avenue S.E., Suite 400, Washington, DC, 20003.

One of the few Canadian firms that conducts custom research is SVP Canada. SVP companies are located in most major countries around the world and provide a free quotation before doing the research. A brochure describing their services can be obtained by writing to the firm at 144 Front Street West, Toronto, Ontario, M5J 2L7 or telephoning (416) 593-5211.

Academic
Libraries

If by some miracle you and a reference librarian have exhausted every possible source of information available in the public library system, you may find answers to your questions in an academic library. (School libraries are not discussed in this chapter, because they represent collections that are only of use to elementary and high school students.) Two types of academic libraries exist. There are about 150 *college* libraries and 110 *university* libraries in Canada, according to Statistics Canada.

Your public librarian may refer you to either. Some college libraries have extremely sophisticated information sources in some areas. For example, if you were researching the fur trade industry or darkroom techniques, a community college offering programs in those areas might very well have a wealth of data available. Larger libraries may also have some of this information, but if you live in a remote part of the country, it may be more expedient for you to contact your nearest college library.

Your local librarian is the key adviser in directing you to outside libraries. Have her or him call the other library for you and arrange an appointment. For a list of college and university libraries, refer to the *Canadian Library Handbook*.

Special   If, after searching through the public library
Libraries   system and academic libraries, you still
                 haven't solved your information needs, a li-
brarian may refer you to a special library. Special libraries are not in
most instances supported by tax dollars; their sole purpose is to meet
an organization's *internal* needs. However, you may be able to gain
access to a special library with the help of a referral from another
librarian.

The general procedure is to go through your local library, because
special librarians are very familiar with the holdings of the public
library system. If you request information that is already obtainable
in the public system, don't expect a special library to help you.

There are an estimated 1,500 to 2,000 special libraries in Canada,
some of which were formed in the mid-nineteenth century. This
includes government special libraries. Although these libraries, too,
service their own organizations, they can also be a resource; special
librarians may feel obligated to help outsiders, because public tax
dollars are involved.

To locate the special libraries closest to you, refer to the *Canadian
Library Handbook*. If you live in Toronto, Montreal, Calgary, or
Edmonton, your local public library should keep a directory of all
special libraries in your city.

Special libraries do not resemble traditional libraries. Their book
collections are often limited, and most of their information comes
from computer services and the telephone. Special librarians form a
very strong network with each other, particularly when they share
similar subject areas. This is partly because of economic necessity
and is most often the case in company libraries, where budget
cutbacks have taken their toll. Special librarians have helped each
other through tough economic times by offering free advice and
exchanging various information services. This network has obvious
advantages for you. If you establish contact with *one* special librarian, you are in effect tapping into a wider network.

To sum up, many special librarians will help you providing you
have a legitimate research need that cannot be met by the public
library system. A lot depends on the librarian's workload, so it pays
to telephone the library first and allow ample time to set up an
information search.

Accessing Local
Government Sources

Chapter Fifteen

"What is strange about the municipal level of government is that it's usually the most open level, because it's (politically) non-partisan. Because of this, it tends to be less difficult to get information."

Barbara Caplan, Deputy Clerk, City of Toronto

Do you want to find out how many dogs Sir John A. Macdonald kept at his house while he lived in Toronto? How about finding the home address of someone who has an unlisted telephone number? Perhaps you want to learn all you can about a proposed development in your neighbourhood? Or you may need to know how much you will be taxed for running a local business.

You can answer all of these questions in a flash by visiting your local government—that is, once you survive a gruelling orientation. Local governments may be the most open form of government, but they also tend to be the most confusing in terms of structure and what information you are legally entitled to.

Many people, myself included, have mistakenly thought that "city government" or "city hall" was synonymous with local government. There are, in fact, many other forms of local government. In British Columbia there are six different types of municipal governments, including city governments. In Ontario the structure is even more elaborate and encompasses villages, towns, cities, boroughs, separated towns, townships, improvement districts, police villages, counties, and metropolitan and regional municipalities.

Don't relax yet—that's only the beginning of this myriad. In addition to the various forms of local government, there are also many kinds of local governing bodies—"special-purpose bodies"— such as boards and commissions. In Ontario alone, one survey found 70 different types of special-purpose bodies representing 2,000 local governing bodies.

Local governments have, in fact, been an organizational nightmare since Confederation. Section 92 of the Constitution Act, 1867 (formerly the British North America Act, 1867) places municipalities under provincial jurisdiction; therefore, provincial statutes can create or dissolve local governments.

Legislation Affecting Research	Under the common law in effect throughout Canada except Quebec, the public has absolutely no legal access to local government

information—that's right, *none*. But here's good news: With the introduction of hundreds of pieces of provincial and municipal legislation, a lot of information is now available to us.

It is not always a simple task to comprehend the laws that give us access to information. This area of law is chaotic and cumbersome, and even the courts are struggling to come to grips with it. Therefore, consider the following comments as *guidelines*, rather than rules, for doing research at this level of government.

The main piece of legislation that affects you as a researcher is the *Municipal Act* or equivalent provincial statute. It states in part that anything in the possession of the municipal clerk is public information. In addition, some local governments have passed by-laws specifying what information must be made available to the public and what information can be disposed of. Many special-purpose bodies abide by a totally different set of rules, because they have been created by different provincial departments. (Special-purpose bodies are discussed in more detail on pages 108 and 109.)

Studying the pertinent legislation is not absolutely necessary, but if your research needs consistently involve municipal sources, it is worthwhile. For the occasional user it may be unnecessarily confusing. In Ontario, for instance, the Municipal Act states, with certain exceptions, that *records*, *books*, *documents*, and *accounts* in the possession of the clerk must be made available for public inspection. Other provinces have similar provisions. These terms, however, are open to a lot of interpretation; there have been legal wranglings over how generic a term like "record" or "document" is, and a few court cases have ensued. Also, the Ontario legislation doesn't explain that only *factual* information, such as minutes of council, by-laws, and resolutions, is public. Excluded are internal staff documents, such as municipal staff reports that might not be discussed in council or reports by the solicitors for the local government.

Don't let this deter you. This chapter will show you that a lot of information can be retrieved without expert knowledge of the legislation. However, an understanding of the laws can help you if you are in that rare situation where you are being denied information.

Information
Available from
Local Sources

If you've never used your local government to obtain information, be aware of what you're missing. Local governments, after all, are involved in virtually every area of your life and store an infinite range of information. Just ponder the tremendous scope of local government authority: Municipal governments pave roads and remove the snow from them, collect and dispose of garbage, administer and often operate public transportation systems, provide police and fire protection, handle building and plumbing inspection, and provide a wide range of services, from day care to parks. Local government may also license over a hundred types of businesses. Its powers allow it to dictate how you can develop your property and how your neighbourhood can develop. These are only a few of its activities.

The kinds of information you can access are just as impressive. Much of it isn't available in published form but rather in records and files. The information you seek is kept on file for varying lengths of time and can be stored in any number of places in a municipality.

Beginning
Your Research

Where do you begin your search for information? It is advisable to arm yourself with a rudimentary knowledge of the structure of your local government. This makes it far easier to find specific kinds

of information. For instance, if you're searching for a health régula-
tion and you know there is a health department, you won't waste
your time approaching the building department. Some local governments publish organizational manuals listing departments and officials and their areas of authority. If there isn't one available in your
area, you can write to the municipal clerk, asking for the name of the
department that can best meet your needs.

A good, quick guide to understanding the types of local governments in your province is Volume Two of *The Source Book: The
Corpus Almanac,* found in your public library. In a page or two the
editor unravels the local government structure of each province;
included are the names and addresses of the municipal clerks.

The clerk is perhaps the most knowledgeable official in any local
government. The clerk's powers, which are provided for in the
provincial Municipal Acts, include recording the minutes of council
and retaining various kinds of information.

Begin by writing to the local clerk, outlining as precisely as
possible what it is you wish to know. You might want to find out, for
instance, how to apply for a business licence. I advise writing or
telephoning, as opposed to showing up in person unannounced—it
usually yields better results. If you visit a municipal department
demanding information that can take the staff two solid days to
obtain, you may be told the information is not available. This
shouldn't come as a surprise. And don't interpret the denial as a case
of government secrecy. Municipal governments, like other institutions, have been affected by budget cutbacks, and there is only so
much their staffs can accomplish at once. Keep this in mind, and
your information search will proceed much more smoothly.

Telephoning the government is not always desirable, either,
especially large municipal governments, because it can be difficult to
reach the clerk. Putting your request in writing makes life easier for
the staff. The clerk usually reroutes your letter to the correct
department or replies with advice about where to find the information you need. By writing, you also minimize your chances of being
denied information, because the staff has to put the denial in writing
and state a reason. It's generally easier to honour your request.

I have singled out the clerk as a key employee. If, however, you
are fortunate enough to live in a municipality with a local archives,
you can also contact the archivist. He or she usually knows everything there is to know about the kinds of information available from
the municipality and how to access them.

When the
Doors Close

You may encounter a situation where a local government official refuses to allow you to inspect records. Sometimes this is the result of wording your request improperly. Here is an example of a poorly worded request: "Will you give me the name of the company that applied for the licence to run the dog kennel down the street?" The government official may not tell you, because the the Municipal Act and corresponding acts say that you may *inspect*, and obtain copies of, documents—nothing is mentioned about offering verbal information. This is a better way to get that information: "May I inspect the licence of the dog kennel down the street?" A request worded in this way also produces better results, because in most municipalities the information is in the possession of the clerk, and the public therefore has the right to examine it.

Here's another example of an incorrect approach: You write to the clerk of the City of Toronto requesting copies of documents that show the election expenses of elected officials. The City of Toronto does not legally require local politicians to file this information, but most of them do. Some of these politicians have asked the clerk's department that copies of these documents not be made available to the public. The correct approach is to ask to *inspect* the records—and you would be allowed to do so. And you won't be stopped if you want to photograph or make notes of them.

If you encounter a situation where you are flatly denied access to some information in the clerk's possession, ask the official to identify the provincial statute or regulations, or local government by-laws, prohibiting you from seeing the material. If the official cannot answer this question, point out that the Municipal Act (or equivalent provincial statute) states that certain kinds of information in the clerk's possession must be made available for public inspection. (But keep in mind that the information you seek may for some reason be exempt from this and other acts.)

If you are still denied access to a document or record that you feel you have a legal right to view, you can take your local government to County Court, requesting an order, called *mandamus*, to make the document available to you.

That's exactly what happened in April, 1974, when a local resident and taxpayer took the City of Timmins to court, because he had been denied certified copies of the municipal accounts. He argued that he was legally entitled to the invoices and vouchers because the Municipal Act stated that all information in possession of the clerk was public—and he won. Similar cases have resulted in other municipalities introducing freedom of information by-laws, detailing what the public is allowed to see.

There hasn't been a flood of these cases throughout Canada, because most citizens don't use local governments as a source of information unless they are directly affected by an issue. Those who do often end their search unnecessarily when they're denied information. To repeat: If you're being denied information, take the matter a few steps further—chances are you will succeed. After all, like you, the government would rather avoid the messy business of litigation unless a grand principle is involved.

Special-Purpose
Bodies

When you deal with special-purpose bodies, you may sometimes be unable to find statutes explaining what information you have a right to, and sometimes you may discover that a special-purpose body has an unwritten policy. The municipality's legal department can help clarify these policies.

For instance, I once wanted basic information on a few questionable Toronto companies. In Toronto, unlike most Canadian municipalities, a special-purpose body, the Metro Licensing Commission, regulates and licenses most Toronto businesses. It was set up by the Ontario government as a kind of consumer protection service, similar in function to the Better Business Bureau, and there are no statutory requirements compelling it to make information available to the public. I was told by the commission that I wouldn't be given any information, other than whether the companies held business licences and whether there were any complaints on file. I wouldn't be given any details of these complaints, nor would even basic information, such as the address of a company, be forthcoming. The employee at the commission insisted that I would be told nothing more unless I was an interested party involved in an accident or lawsuit.

The Metropolitan Toronto legal department, however, said otherwise. The lawyer in charge of handling decisions for the commission informed me that the commission has an unwritten policy that the public has a right to inspect a company's address, names of directors (if they are on file), and licence number. (The full application form for a business licence cannot be inspected, because it may contain information about a person's criminal record; the municipality could be sued for disclosing such information.) The public also has the right to inspect minutes of the commission's meetings and, possibly, the minutes of any special hearings dealing with applications for a licence under unusual circumstances. This is obviously far more information than the first government official had said was available to me.

Documents Available for Public Inspection   By this time you are probably interested to learn exactly *what* information is available to the general public. As I have stressed throughout this chapter, this varies considerably from province to province and depends on how you conduct your information search. While you have a legal right to certain information in every province, some local governments give more than is legally required, and others don't give you the minimum amount of information you are entitled to unless you take the matter to court. The following are some of the kinds of records (out of hundreds of potential records) that can usually be obtained and that have assisted me in my own research.

Council Minutes   Every municipality keeps minutes of its council meetings and makes them available to you on request. The quality of the minutes varies widely. In some cases the council of the municipality requests that the clerk keep full minutes, similar to *Hansard* (the transcript of the debates of the House of Commons). From such minutes you can learn how a decision evolved and what opinions were expressed by the council members. On the other hand, the minutes may be very sketchy and contain little more than what decisions were made. Minutes are sometimes printed in both English and French.

A word of caution: If you are looking for resolutions or by-laws, keep in mind that an amendment to them may have been adopted at a later meeting. Also, check the appendix of the minutes for any documents or studies that were discussed at council meetings and that may be included.

Policy Decisions of Special-Purpose Bodies   Your local clerk can tell you which special-purpose bodies operate in your area. You may, for example, want to find out what a library board's policy is on shelving children's books. Or perhaps you want to know who is allowed to drive a taxi in your municipality. In many cases the meetings and minutes of a special-purpose body are open to the public.

School Support Lists   Most municipalities keep these computer-ized lists to keep track of who financially supports the public and separate school systems. The information is compiled by the provin-cial government and is organized alphabetically by surname. These lists can be highly useful if you want to trace someone. For example, I once wanted to find the home address of Gordon Lightfoot. Lightfoot is one of Canada's most popular entertainers and is naturally a private person with an unlisted telephone number. But the 1976 school support lists for the City of Toronto made it possible to find his address.

   Practically everyone's name appears on school support lists. Other information includes all properties they own, whether they are a Canadian citizen (or other British subject) or alien, whether they live at the address shown, and whether they are the owner of the building or a tenant.

   School support lists are kept in different departments, depending on the local government. The City of Toronto keeps them in its archives.

Tax Assessment Rolls   These are compiled by provincial govern-ments for tax purposes, in this case to assess land taxes. They're generally arranged by address and indicate if the owner or tenant resides at the location; they also give the dimensions of the property. Older (pre-1970s) tax assessment rolls contain much more informa-tion, including a person's occupation, number of children, and if you go back to before the turn of the century, the number of cattle, dogs, and horses the person owned!

Voters' Lists   These are kept for each level of government. At the local level, they are arranged by street and compiled whenever there is a municipal election. They list who lives at an address, whether the person is married, and whether he or she is an owner or tenant. Voters' lists provide another method of tracing someone, provided of course that you have some indication of which neighbourhood a person lives in.

Building Permit Records   You won't be able to look at the floor plans for a local bank, but you can probably inspect standard building permit applications that have been approved. Table 15.1 shows such an application; you can see the typical kinds of information that must be filed, including the property owner's name, address, and telephone number. It's a handy source for tracing an elusive landlord!

Committee of Adjustment Records　These records are similar to building permits. The two-sided form, reproduced in Table 15.2, must be completed by property owners who wish to be exempt from local by-laws when altering a building. They must provide their name, address, telephone number, and the names and addresses of any mortgagees.

Local Politicians' Files　In some municipalities local politicians (including, but not only, aldermen) may donate their files to the municipality once they retire. These files can provide a wealth of information on countless subjects. Most of it has been prepared by expert staff researchers, not necessarily by the local politicians themselves. Take advantage of this information.

Archives　As mentioned on page 106, some municipalities keep an archives. If this is true of your local government, make an appointment to visit this department. The City of Toronto archives, one of the best in North America, has an extensive collection of records on every topic affecting Torontonians. This includes files donated by special-interest groups, photographs, maps, artifacts, and much more.

Records of Back Taxes and Work Orders　This kind of information is much more difficult for the public to obtain. For example, land taxes owed on a property or violations of city by-laws are two kinds of information that are generally available only to a lawyer acting for a prospective home buyer. However, it may be valuable enough to you to hire a lawyer to obtain it for you.

Water Bills　You may be able to find out if a homeowner has paid his or her water bill. This information, which can indicate a person's financial stability, can sometimes be obtained verbally from the Water Revenue Branch or equivalent department.

TABLE 15.1   Sample Municipal Building Department Application

PERMIT APPLICATION

Please type or print

MUNICIPAL NUMBER (S)	PROPERTY ADDRESS	

TYPE OF WORK

☐ Building ☐ H.V.A.C. ☐ Plumbing/Drainage ☐ Exterior Signage ☐ Demolition

EXISTING USE OF PROPERTY	NO. OF DWELLING UNITS

PROPOSED USE OF PROPERTY	NO. OF DWELLING UNITS

DESCRIPTION OF WORK

☐ Build ☐ Interior Alterations ☐ Additions ☐ Change of Occupancy ☐ Demolish   HUDAC NO. :|_|_|_|_|_|_|_|

Please give details _____

ESTIMATED COST OF PROPOSED WORK	NUMBER OF STOREYS		CONSTRUCTION TYPE
$	ABOVE GRADE	BELOW GRADE	☐ Combustible ☐ Non-Combustible

NAME OF OWNER	TELEPHONE

ADDRESS	(POSTAL CODE)

NAME OF APPLICANT	TELEPHONE

ADDRESS	(POSTAL CODE)

FOR OFFICE USE ONLY

FEES:

$ _____ EXAMINATION + $ _____ SURVEY + $ _____ WATER = $ _____ TOTAL

☐ PART 3   ☐ PART 6   ☐ PART 8   ☐ PART 9

SEWER IMPOST: ☐ YES ☐ NO   FIELD REVIEW REQUIRED: ☐ YES ☐ NO   CITY TEAM:

I, _____ do solemnly declare:

1. That I am the owner/authorized agent of the owner named in the above application for a permit.
2. That the plans and specifications submitted are prepared for the work described in the permit application.
3. That the information supplied by me in the application and in the materials filed by me with the application is correct.
4. That the proper legal name(s) of the registered owner(s) of the property is/are:
   (strike out if applicant is authorized agent)

4. That to the best of my knowledge, information and belief the proper legal name(s) of the registered owner(s) of the property is/are:
   (strike out if applicant is owner)

And I make this Solemn Declaration conscientiously believing it to be true, and knowing it is of the same force and effect as if made under oath and by virtue of "The Canada Evidence Act".

Applicant's
Signature: _____

Declared before me

this _____ day of _____ in the year 19 _____ .

A Notary Public Commissioner, etc. _____

My Commission expires on: _____

Please note:

All dimensions are to be given either in square feet OR metres.   Please indicate which you are using: ☐ sq. ft. ☐ m.

REVISIONS TO FEES		
EXAMINATION FEE	**WATER FEES**	**OTHER CHARGES**
No. of ☐ sq. ft. ☐ m _____	_____ = _____	**SEWER:**
Cost per ☐ sq. ft. ☐ m $ _____	_____ = _____	Gross Floor Area _____ ☐ sq. ft ☐ m
	_____ = _____	Exemption _____
REVISED FEES:	_____ = _____	Balance _____
Revised Cost $ _____		Charge @ ____ ¢ per ☐ sq. ft. ☐ m $ _____
Revised Fee $ _____	Sub-Total $ _____	
Fee Paid $ _____	Special Sewer Charge _____ % _____	per _____
Balance Due $ _____	Less _____ % _____	
	TOTAL WATER CHARGE:	**SURVEY:**
	$ _____	Examination Fee $ _____
per _____	per _____	per _____

ZONING APPROVAL		TECHNICAL APPROVAL	
SIGNATURE	DATE	SIGNATURE	DATE
SIGNATURE	DATE	SIGNATURE	DATE

TABLE 15.2   Sample Application for Exemption from a Municipal By-Law

APPLICATION FOR MINOR VARIANCE OR FOR PERMISSION

The undersigned hereby applies to the Committee of Adjustment under section 44 of The Planning Act, 1983, for relief, as described in this application, from By-law No. _____

1   Name of Owner:

2   Address: Postal Code:

    Telephone   (home):   (business):

3   Name of Agent (if any):

4   Address: Postal Code:

    Telephone   (home):   (business):

5   Names and addresses of any mortgagees, holders of charges or other encumbrancers, please include postal code:

6   Nature and extent of relief applied for:

7   Why is it not possible to comply with the provisions of the By-law?

8   Legal description of subject lands (registered plan number and lot number or other legal description and, where applicable, street and number):

9   Dimensions of lands affected:

    Frontage: Depth: Area: Width of Street:

10   Particulars of all buildings on or proposed for the subject lands, (specify ground floor area, gross floor area, number of storeys, width, length, height, etc.):

    Existing: _____

    Proposed: _____

11 Location of all buildings and structures on or proposed for the subject lands, (specify distance from side, rear and front lot lines):

Existing: _____

_____

Proposed: _____

12 Date of acquisition of subject lands:

13 Date of construction of all buildings and structures on subject lands: _____

14 Existing uses of the subject property: _____

15 Existing uses of abutting properties: _____

16 Length of time the existing uses of the subject property have continued:

17 Municipal services available (check appropriate box(es):

☐ Water   ☐ Connected   ☐ Sanitary Sewers   ☐ Connected   ☐ Storm Sewers

18 Present Official Plan provisions applying to the land: _____

19 Present Restricted Area By-law (Zoning By-law) provisions applying to the land: _____

20 Has the owner previously applied for relief in respect of the subject property?   ☐ Yes   ☐ No
If the answer is "yes," describe briefly:

_____

_____

_____

21 Is the subject property the subject of a current application for consent under section 49 of the Planning Act?   ☐ Yes   ☐ No

_____
Signature of Applicant or Authorized Agent

Dated at the _____ of _____ this _____ day of _____ 19 ____

I, _____ of the _____ of _____

in the _____ of _____

solemnly declare that: All of the above statements are true, and I make this solemn declaration conscientiously believing it to be true and knowing that it is of the same force and effect as if made under oath.

Declared before me at the

_____ of _____

in the
Judicial District of

_____ this _____

day of _____ A.D. 19 _____

_____

A Commissioner, etc.

Accessing Provincial Government Sources

Chapter Sixteen

Do you want to gather information on a private company to prepare yourself for a job interview? Are you making a loan and need a source of information on the financial stability of either an individual or a company? Are you hiring a chauffeur and need to access a driver's record? Do you need a reliable source to verify someone's marital status, change of name, or death?

You can answer all of these queries using provincial government sources, but it requires sophisticated digging. You may have to study this chapter patiently more than once. In many cases you can obtain this information for under $10.

Provincial governments have a broad mandate. A partial list of their responsibilities includes taxation (as it relates to the provinces), the administering of prisons, natural resources, property, civil rights, marriages, and divorces. A comprehensive list of provincial jurisdictions is found in Section 92 of the Constitution Act, 1867. One thing you can count on: There is a wealth of publicly available information on people and business at this level of government.

Provincial governments are arranged in a myriad of ministries, departments, agencies, boards, commissions, and Crown corporations. Each of these bodies has its own structure and functions.

Locating
Departments
and Civil
Servants

The quickest way to locate the most useful body and civil servant is to telephone the provincial *hotline* in your area. The staffs operating these hotlines, or general inquiry numbers, are trained to refer you to the appropriate place—quickly. The hotline numbers are:

- Yukon Territory: (403) 667-5745.
- Northwest Territories: (403) 873-7442.
- British Columbia: (604) 387-1337.
- Alberta: (403) 427-2754.
- Saskatchewan: (306) 565-6291.
- Manitoba: (204) 944-3744.
- Ontario: (416) 965-3535.
- Quebec: (418) 643-1344.
- New Brunswick: 1-800-561-0123.
- Nova Scotia: (902) 424-6980.
- Prince Edward Island: (902) 892-3428.
- Newfoundland: (709) 737-3610.

These inquiry numbers are handy if you don't know where to start. Be patient: You may have to speak to two or three parties before you reach the civil servant who can help you. If you plan to use provincial government sources on a regular basis, however, familiarize yourself with the directories that help you pinpoint the correct provincial body and, equally important, the most knowledgeable civil servant. The directories discussed below are also used by hotline staff.

Every provincial government has a publisher—often called a Queen's Printer—who distributes provincial publications, such as provincial telephone directories. These directories can be especially helpful. They are generally divided into an alphabetical listing of all the provincial civil servants—from secretaries to cabinet ministers—and a listing of the various bureaucratic bodies, with civil servants listed according to title. Usually a brief description of the responsibilities of the body, and a general inquiry number, are given.

Some provinces also publish a handy complementary volume to the telephone directory that lists key words that refer you to the appropriate body. For example, if you need to find a contact for provincial grants, you would search under the key word "grants."

These directories have different names. In Nova Scotia, for example, it's called *A Guide to the Nova Scotia Government*; in Ontario it's the *Kwic Index*.

Similar, privately published directories can be equally useful. These include *The Source Book: The Corpus Almanac* and *The Corpus Administrative Index* (and its newly published, complementary subject guide that makes the *Index* easier to use). These directories, usually available in any library, can be used for many different purposes. For example, if you want to know the telephone number of the provincial government publisher and bookstore, search under "Government Services" or "Supply and Services." (The only exception is Alberta, where they are listed under "The Public Affairs Bureau.") The *Canadian Almanac and Directory* provides information similar to that in the Corpus publications.

Locating
Provincial
Government
Publications
A wealth of thoroughly researched material has been assembled for the provincial governments by knowledgeable civil servants, hired consultants, private research firms, university project groups, and so on—you just have to know where to find it. Several reference sources can help you, and they are described in the following pages.

Microlog Index   The best reference source is the *Microlog Index*. This is a monthly and annual index published by Micromedia Limited, Toronto, and most public libraries subscribe to it. It sifts through every conceivable government publication, at every level of government, and microfilms and indexes any material with research value.

Micromedia sells the microfilmed reports and studies for a fee. However, first check through the *Microlog Index* in your nearest library, list the materials you want, then find out if they are kept in your library or are easily available from the ministry that produced them or from the government bookstore. If not, write to Micromedia Limited, Document Delivery Department, 144 Front Street West, Toronto, Ontario, M5J 2L7 or telephone (416) 593-5211. A paper copy of a 20-page report costs about $7. A 200-page report costs about $32, and anything longer than that costs an additional 14¢ per page. Microfiche copies are considerably less expensive.

If you can't find the information you're looking for in the *Microlog*

Index, try the other routes described below; they are also used by the Microlog staff, but there is always the chance that something has been omitted.

Bibliographic Checklist   Almost every provincial government publishes a bibliographic checklist of material produced by its different bodies. These include official reports, administrative reports, statistical reports, periodicals, special reports, catalogues, and bibliographies. Most material published by a provincial government is included in these checklists.

The following is a list of the bibliographic checklists for all provinces and territories except the Yukon Territory and Newfoundland, which were undergoing changes at the time of publication of this book:

- The Northwest Territories' *Publications Catalogue* (annual).
- *British Columbia Government Publications Monthly Checklist.*
- Alberta's *Publications Catalogue* (quarterly and annual).
- *Manitoba Government Publications Monthly Checklist.*
- *Checklist of Saskatchewan Government Publications* (monthly) and *Checklist of Saskatchewan Government Publications Annual Cumulation.*
- *Liste mensuelle des publications du gouvernement du Québec* (monthly) and *Liste mensuelle des publications du gouvernement du Québec index des titres de l'année* (annual).
- *Ontario Government Publications Monthly Checklist* and *Ontario Government Publications Annual Catalogue.*
- *New Brunswick Government Publications* (annual).
- *Publications of the Province of Nova Scotia Quarterly Checklist* (also published at the end of each year in one volume).
- *Prince Edward Island Government Publications* (published about every two months).

These lists include most of the material published at the provincial government level. The remainder of the material is more difficult to locate and is found in different places.

Departmental Lists   Departmental lists (or ministry lists) are bibliographies of published materials, quite independent of the checklists previously discussed. These titles may or may not appear on the main checklists. To learn about departmental lists, contact the library of the department concerned and ask to speak with its librarian, or contact the department's communications officer.

Other Lists   Some departments or bodies print lists of all the material they publish. These lists are more up-to-date than the regular provincial checklists—an item may appear on this list three, months before appearing on the checklist. To be included on the mailing list to receive this information is not always easy for the general public. You should be able to offer a valid reason; for example, perhaps you're involved in a business venture that falls under a particular department. Start by contacting either the departmental library or its publicity co-ordinator (sometimes called a communications officer).

Limited Distribution Reports   There are also publications, known as *limited distribution reports*, that aren't included on any type of checklist. These reports or studies are often highly technical or of limited public interest and are classified as limited distribution reports for a number of reasons: The department may think there isn't enough demand to warrant a large print run; the department may want to save money and by classifying the reports as such, it is not required to translate them into French. In other words, the government doesn't label the material in this fashion to hide it but to save money. To learn about these reports, contact the library of the department concerned, or the communications officer or publications co-ordinator.

Canadian News Index   Most major studies or reports, however they are classified, are mentioned in the media. Thus, you can use the *Canadian News Index* at your nearest library as a guide, searching under your subject.

Other Provincial Government Business   If you want to supplement the media coverage of the work of provincial governments, there is a variety of sources at your fingertips. For example, legislative minutes are available at most libraries. Libraries also keep copies of *Provincial Pulse*, published by CCH Canadian Limited, Toronto. This is a loose-leaf publication that appears twice a month and lists all the major activities of each provincial government. *Canadian News Facts* can also be helpful. Published weekly, it provides a synopsis of important news, including information relating to all levels of government. It is indexed quarterly and annually and is kept at most libraries. *Canadian News Facts* is a good source for dates and events, while *Provincial Pulse* and legislative minutes are excellent sources for probing further.

The remainder of this chapter is devoted to key sources of information that are pertinent for gathering data on *people* and *businesses*. They also indicate the scope of information available at this level of government. There are, of course, countless other sources from a vast number of provincial government bodies— enough to fill a book on their own.

If you require sources that are not discussed in the following pages, telephone your provincial government hotline for assistance or search for leads through the directories mentioned.

Business Records	Many kinds of provincial government records give you an insight into the corporate structure and financial stability of companies. Most of

the information is available to the public from the various companies branch offices of the Ministry of Consumer and Commercial Relations or its equivalent department.

When you conduct a company search, keep in mind the three types of businesses in Canada: sole proprietorships (provincially registered, usually owned and operated by a single individual), partnerships (provincially registered and owned by at least two individuals or companies), and corporations (provincially or federally incorporated).

The kinds of information that you can find on each type of business varies considerably from province to province. In some provinces you can conduct a few straightforward searches in a single office and gather all the information you need. But in another province you may have to visit several offices and wade through a variety of different legal documents before you find what you want.

To find out how your provincial department operates, get in touch with the provincial registrar. Ask that official what kinds of business searches are possible in the province and where the information can be obtained. The following is a list of addresses of the provincial registrars across Canada; most of the business searches described later in this chapter can be done directly at these offices:

Yukon Territory
Territorial Secretary and Registrar General
P. O. Box 2703
Government of the Yukon Territory
Whitehorse, Yukon
Y1A 2C6
Telephone: (403) 667-5442
Telex: 036-8260

Northwest Territories
Registrar of Companies
Legal Registry
Department of Justice and Public Services
Government of the Northwest Territories
Yellowknife, Northwest Territories
X1A 2L9
Telephone: (403) 873-7492
Telex: 034-45528

British Columbia
Ministry of Consumer and Corporate Affairs
Corporate and Central Registry
940 Blanshard Street
Victoria, British Columbia
V8W 3E6
Telephone: (604) 387-5101
Telex: 049-7351

Alberta
Companies Branch
Alberta Consumer and Corporate Affairs
9803–102A Avenue
14th Floor
Edmonton, Alberta
T5J 3A3
Telephone: (403) 427-4064
Telex: 037-41848
TWX 610-831-942

Saskatchewan
Corporations Branch

Saskatchewan Consumer and Commercial Affairs
Third Floor, 2121 Saskatchewan Drive
Regina, Saskatchewan
S4P 3V7
Telephone: (306) 565-2962

Manitoba
Consumer and Corporate Affairs
10th Floor
405 Broadway Avenue
Woodsworth Building
Winnipeg, Manitoba
R3C 3L6
Telephone: (204) 945-2500

Ontario
Companies Services Branch
Letters Search Department
Ministry of Consumer and Commercial Relations
555 Yonge Street
Toronto, Ontario
M7A 2H6
Telephone: (416) 963-0552

Quebec
Direction des compagnies
L'Inspecteur général des institutions financières
800, place D'Youville
5e étage
Québec, Québec
G1R 4Y5
Telephone: (418) 643-5253
Telex: 051-3706

Quebec (Montreal office)
Direction des compagnies
L'Inspecteur général des institutions financières
800, place Victoria
42e étage, Bureau 4208
Case Postale 246
Montréal, Québec 246

H4Z 1G3
Telephone: (514) 873-5324

New Brunswick
Department of Justice
Consumer and Corporate Affairs
P. O. Box 6000
Fredericton, New Brunswick
E3B 5H1
Telephone: (506) 453-2703
Telex: 014-46230

Nova Scotia
Registrar of Joint Stock Companies
Department of the Attorney General
1660 Hollis Street
P. O. Box 1529
Halifax, Nova Scotia
B3J 2Y4
Telephone: (902) 424-7770
Telex: 019-22884

Prince Edward Island
Corporations Division
Department of Justice
P. O. Box 2000
Charlottetown, Prince Edward Island
C1A 7N8
Telephone: (902) 892-5411
Telex: 014-44154

Newfoundland
Registry of Deeds, Companies and Securities
Department of Justice
P. O. Box 4750
Confederation Building
St. John's, Newfoundland
A1C 5T7
Telephone: (709) 737-2591

A list of the general types of business searches that can be done are discussed in the next few pages. Because the laws governing businesses in each province are different, you will encounter different types of legal documents that must be filed with the provincial government and different names for the departments that handle this information.

The contents of the searches are *for the most part* the same across Canada, but the form the information takes varies considerably from province to province; therefore, these descriptions cannot be applied identically everywhere. They represent the basic kinds of searches for most provinces. Contact your provincial registrar for further details. Of course, these searches represent *provincial* sources only. There are also federal and court records, and these are discussed in Chapters 17 and 18.

A provincial business search, as I mentioned, can usually be conducted at the office of the registrar. It can take from a few hours to several days to conduct one search, depending on the complexity of the company records and the workload of the staff who handle public queries. Some provinces allow the public to place their requests by telephone and then pick up the information when it is ready. A small fee (usually under $5) is charged for most searches, excluding photocopying fees; in most provinces you can set up an account if you plan to do business searches on a regular basis.

Securities Commission Records   Compiling information about public companies is in many ways easier than about private companies. Public companies in Canada are those that raise capital by offering shares to the public. These shares are generally issued by companies through securities underwriters and are in turn sold to the public. Shares are often listed later on stock exchanges. In Canada stock exchanges are found in Toronto, Montreal, Winnipeg, Alberta, and Vancouver.

Public companies are governed by various provincial securities statutes and must make available to the public certain kinds of information to protect their shareholders. This information includes: a prospectus (explaining how the company is structured and what it does); any press releases; regular, audited financial statements; *insider reports* (listing any insider shareholders—those who own 10 per cent or more of a company—and any director or officer who owns shares); annual reports; debt structure (which reveals the company's borrowing habits and what assets are tied up by a secured loan); and a list of subsidiary companies.

If the company sells public shares in the United States, it must file even more detailed information with the U.S. Securities and Exchange Commission (SEC). Some of the SEC information may also be included in provincial securities commission files. You may find, for instance, Form 10-K, which is a detailed annual report of a company giving information on such things as its products and services, markets, a list of its properties, any pending legal proceedings, five-year financial data, and sometimes the salaries of its directors and officers. An SEC Form 10-Q may also be included in provincial records. It provides an updated financial outlook since the previous Form 10-K was filed.

If you are researching a major public company, chances are that its shares are listed on a stock exchange. If so, you can probably inspect the documents discussed above at the stock exchange itself, free of charge. If you're not sure which public company is listed on what stock exchange, check a major daily newspaper in your area. The financial pages list all the stock exchanges and what companies trade on them. You then know what province to refer to.

You may, however, require information on a public company that is not listed on a stock exchange. Stocks of such companies are traded on an "unlisted market" (or "over the counter"). To research such companies, as well as companies that are listed on stock exchanges, you can do a provincial securities commission search. To do so, you must generally fill out a simple form listing the company's name. Ask for the *general file* and an *insider file* in order to obtain all the publicly available information. Some provinces print an index to the documents that are on file. For example, in Ontario the *OSC Bulletin*, which appears weekly with a cumulative index every six months, lists all documents filed with the Ontario Securities Commission.

In most provinces a small fee is charged for doing a securities commission search. But in Quebec you can view the documents, or be given the information over the telephone, free of charge.

Corporate Search   You can gather various kinds of basic information on any provincially registered corporation—as well as corporations registered in other provinces and federally registered corporations doing business in that province—by doing a corporate search. A straight corporate search provides such information as the correct name of the corporation and any *style* or *trade names* it uses for conducting business with the public, a list of directors and officers of the company, their addresses, any registered changes in this information, the date of incorporation, and in many instances the structure of the corporation, and if and how the shares are offered.

In some provinces, such as Nova Scotia and Ontario, a corporate search gives you only skeletal information on a business. On the other hand, a corporate search in British Columbia provides considerably more, including information on encumbrances. *Encumbrances* include various kinds of debentures and can help to determine the indebtedness or borrowing habits of a company. Encumbrances are detailed enough to show you what personal property assets (equipment and anything other than land or buildings) are tied up in a loan.

Most provinces require you to fill out a form listing the corporate name and provincial corporation number of the corporation you're researching. You can find this number by using the microfiche reader in the provincial office, free of charge, and scanning the set of microfiche that is usually kept beside the reader. These fiche contain an alphabetical list of all corporations registered in that province, including any corporations registered in another province that have an "extra-provincial" licence to operate in the province and any federally registered corporations conducting business there. The fiche list the corporate name and date of incorporation.

If you can't find the name, it may be that the business is federally incorporated and is not operating in that province, or it may be a provincially registered sole proprietorship or partnership, or it could be using another name. It is also possible, in a rare instance, that the name you are searching for has not yet been included on the fiche. (To be certain, request the information without providing a corporation number. Some provinces provide you with a corporate search file even if you don't include the corporate number. The number is used to speed up your request.)

A corporate search varies in cost, although the fee is generally a nominal one. There's no charge in Quebec, and it is one of the only provinces to offer a corporate search to anyone over the telephone.

Business Style Search   A *style* or *trade name* is the name a company uses to carry on business with the public. Sometimes a corporation uses one name for the public and another, corporate name for government filings.

To do a business style search, simply fill out a form at the provincial office, providing the style name. You receive a photocopy of the style registration card, which gives the name of the corporation, and then you have to follow this up with a corporate search.

A corporate search provides you with a list of all the style names the business is using. If you don't have the corporate name, but you have the style name, you must do a business style search first.

There is a time frame in which the registration of style names remains valid. If a business doesn't apply to renew the registration of its style name, the previous application form is removed from the file and sent into storage—in some provinces into the provincial archives. You must then apply to the archives to obtain the information.

Sole Proprietorship Search   A sole proprietorship search provides the name and address of the sole proprietor, the nature of the business, and when it began.

To do a sole proprietorship search in most provinces, you fill out a form providing the name of the business. In Quebec the procedure is different, because it is governed by civil law instead of English common law, like the rest of the provinces. In Quebec the first step is to contact the Montreal or Quebec City office responsible for company records. A telephone call is sufficient to obtain the proper name of the sole proprietorship, the name and address of the owner, and the date the business was registered. For further details you must contact the local district courthouse where the firm was registered. Sometimes you can do this over the telephone. The local courthouse in that district can inform you of the marital status of the firm's owner, the name of the owner's spouse (including the maiden name of his wife if the owner is male), where the couple was married, whether or not they are separated, if they are divorced, the court handling the divorce, and the writ number. (With the writ number you can go to the appropriate court and look up the divorce records, which would reveal any settlements.) In some cases the firm search in Quebec also provides the social insurance number of the business owner.

Partnership Search   The partnership search, also conducted at the provincial office responsible for business records, provides a list of the business partners, their addresses, and the date of registration of the business. It may be that several corporations own the business, in which case you have to do a corporate search on each corporation.

Personal Property Security Act Search   Various provincial statutes, such as the Personal Property Security Act (PPSA), enable creditors to register security agreements involving personal property. (Real property, such as land and anything erected on the land, is registered at land registry offices and is discussed later in this chapter.) The kinds of security agreements registered vary widely from province to province.

Ontario, Manitoba, Saskatchewan, and the Yukon have a PPSA, and some of the other provinces are moving in this direction. PPSA offices keep a record of registered *financing statements* (which constitute *notice* of a security agreement) and related *financing change statements* involving personal property for *individuals* and *businesses*. These include various kinds of security agreements, such as chattel mortgages, conditional sales contracts, assignments of book debts, and bonds. Sometimes you come across a notice of a document labelled simply "general security agreement."

All of these terms describe security agreements registered by creditors to protect their interests. They offer different terms, depending on the type of contract involved; what is common to all of them is that a creditor has some legal right to the assets of an individual or a business (excluding, as already noted, real property).

Because the PPSA is a *notice-filing* system, you cannot obtain a copy of the security agreement. However, if you are a debtor, an execution creditor, or have an interest in the collateral, you have a right to a copy of the security agreement or information concerning the amount of the indebtedness, and to obtain it, you must send a request in writing to the secured party.

If you require information on security agreements registered in a province without a Personal Property Security Act, you have to search for this type of information under different legislation, such as an Assignment of Book Debts Act.

To see how relatively easy it is to access PPSA records, look at Table 16.1, which shows a sample enquiry request form. To search for a company's security agreements, check Box D in Part I and provide the name of the business. To obtain a verbal response (the cheapest and quickest way of obtaining the information), check Box A in Part II. If you want to search for an individual debtor, check Box C of Part I.

TABLE 16.1   Sample Enquiry Request Form

ENQUIRY REQUEST

(This form may be duplicated and used to submit written enquiries to the Central Office)

PRINT (BLOCK LETTERS ONLY) OR
TYPE (CAPITAL LETTERS ONLY)

WARNING

If you are making an INDIVIDUAL SPECIFIC or NON-SPECIFIC ENQUIRY, please read pages 2 and 3 of the Debtor Name Enquiry Guide.

If you are making a MOTOR VEHICLE ENQUIRY, please read pages 6 and 7 of the Motor Vehicle Enquiry Guide.

DATE: _____

PART I   COMPLETE A, B, C, OR D TO SHOW TYPE OF ENQUIRY REQUIRED

(COMPLETE ONE FORM FOR EACH ENQUIRY)

A ☐   MOTOR VEHICLE SERIAL NUMBER ENQUIRY

SERIAL NUMBER

B ☐   INDIVIDUAL NON SPECIFIC DEBTOR NAME ENQUIRY

FIRST NAME   SURNAME (LAST NAME)

C ☐   INDIVIDUAL SPECIFIC DEBTOR NAME ENQUIRY

FIRST NAME   INITIAL   SURNAME (LAST NAME)   DATE OF BIRTH
DAY   MONTH   YEAR

D ☐   BUSINESS DEBTOR NAME ENQUIRY

BUSINESS, CORPORATE, PARTNERSHIP OF OTHER NAME (AS APPROPRIATE)

PART II   COMPLETE A, B, OR C TO SHOW TYPE OF RESPONSE REQUIRED

A ☐   VERBAL (FEE $2.00)

B ☐   UNCERTIFIED (PRINTED) (FEE $2.00)

C ☐   CERTIFICATE (FEE $10.00)

PLEASE MAKE YOUR CHEQUE PAYABLE TO:
TREASURER OF ONTARIO

PART III   COMPLETE TO SHOW MALING ADDRESS FOR RESPONSE

NAME (COMPANY OR INDIVIDUAL)   ATTENTION (IF APPLICABLE)

STREET ADDRESS

CITY, TOWN, ETC.   PROVINCE   POSTAL CODE

PPSR 213B 10512

The information requested in the Financing Statement, shown in Table 16.2, is the extent of the information one can retrieve in a PPSA search.

TABLE 16.2   Sample Financing Statement

FINANCING STATEMENT

Form 1B

◄ 12 PITCH
CAREFULLY ALIGN TYPEWRITER
◄ 10 PITCH

REGISTRATION NUMBER (FILING OFFICE USE ONLY)

YR/MTH/DAY   HOUR/MINUTE   BRANCH OFFICE   SEQUENCE

Ministry of
Consumer and
Commercial
Ontario Relations

83- 939706

TYPE "X" IF INSUFFICIENT SPACE
CAUTION FILING
COMPLETE ADDITIONAL
STATEMENTS AND SHOW

01   THIS IS PAGE NUMBER   TOTAL PAGES REQUIRED
OF

DEBTOR

02   SHOW ONE DEBTOR NAME

DATE OF BIRTH   DAY MONTH YEAR   SEX M/F   INDIVIDUAL DEBTOR: FIRST NAME   INITIAL   SURNAME (LAST NAME)

BUSINESS DEBTOR: BUSINESS, CORPORATE, PARTNERSHIP OR OTHER NAME (AS APPROPRIATE)

ADDRESS   CITY, TOWN, ETC.   PROV.

02   COMPLETE LINES 02 & 04
03   OR
04   LINES 03 & 04

DEBTOR

05   SHOW ADDITIONAL DEBTOR NAME (IF ANY)

DATE OF BIRTH   DAY MONTH YEAR   SEX M/F   INDIVIDUAL DEBTOR: FIRST NAME   INITIAL   SURNAME (LAST NAME)

BUSINESS DEBTOR: BUSINESS, CORPORATE, PARTNERSHIP OR OTHER NAME (AS APPROPRIATE)

ADDRESS – IF DIFFERENT FROM ABOVE   CITY, TOWN, ETC.   PROV.

05   IF ADDITIONAL DEBTOR NAME IS SHOWN COMPLETE
06   LINE 05 OR
07   LINE 06

08   SECURED PARTY

NAME

ADDRESS   CITY, TOWN, ETC.   PROV.

08   COMPLETE LINE 08 AND
09   LINE 09

COMPLETE SECTIONS 1 AND 2   COMPLETE SECTIONS 3 AND 4 IF COLLATERAL IS CLASSIFIED AS CONSUMER GOODS

COLLATERAL

SECTION 1. COLLATERAL CLASSIFICATION (TYPE "X" IN AT LEAST ONE BOX)   SECTION 2: MOTOR VEHICLE OR MOTORIZED SNOW VEHICLE INCLUDED IN COLLATERAL (TYPE "X" IN ONE BOX)   SECTION 3:   SECTION 4:

CONSUMER GOODS   INVENTORY   EQUIPMENT   BOOK DEBTS   OTHER   YES   NO   PRINCIPAL AMOUNT SECURED   DATE OF MATURITY DAY MONTH YEAR   TYPE "X" IF NO FIXED MATURITY DATE

10   A   B   C   D   E   F   G   S   .   .   .00   OR

11   MOTOR VEHICLE OR MOTORIZED SNOW VEHICLE DESCRIPTION MUST BE SHOWN
12   IF CLASSIFIED AS CONSUMER GOODS

YR   MAKE   BODY STYLE   SERIAL NUMBER

13   GENERAL COLLATERAL DESCRIPTION (OPTIONAL)
14
15

13   GENERAL COLLATERAL DESCRIPTION (OPTIONAL)
14
15

AGENT

16   REGISTERING AGENT (IF OTHER THAN SECURED PARTY)
17

NAME

ADDRESS   CITY, TOWN, ETC.   PROV.

16   REGISTERING AGENT (IF OTHER THAN SECURED PARTY)
17

AUTHORIZED SIGNATURE

NAME AND SIGNATURE OF SECURED PARTY
– OR –
NAME OF SECURED PARTY AND NAME AND SIGNATURE OF AGENT OF SECURED PARTY

BRANCH FILING OFFICE COPY

REGISTRANT   DO NOT DETACH YOUR COPY IF YOU WISH IT RETURNED (SHOWING REGISTRATION NUMBER). IF YOU WISH THE "REGISTRANT'S COPY" OF THIS STATEMENT TO BE RETURNED TO YOU BY MAIL YOU MUST PROVIDE A SELF ADDRESSED STAMPED ENVELOPE, MINIMUM SIZE 229 mm x 305 mm (OR 9" X 12"). IF YOU DO NOT PROVIDE THE ENVELOPE THE COPY WILL BE DESTROYED.

ANY REPRINTING OF THIS FORM MUST HAVE PRIOR APPROVAL OF THE REGISTRAR

10419 (ED 04/83)

Here is an example of the information you can be given over the telephone upon request for a PPSA verbal search concerning a business I'll call Smith Enterprises:

> The address is 115 Main Street, Rainy River, Ontario. The secured party is Bank of Ontario, 121 Main Street, Rainy River, Ontario. The collateral classification is equipment; a motor vehicle is included; the principal amount secured is $1,565; and there is no fixed date of maturity. The motor vehicle is described on line 11 as a 1972 Impala, serial number 72B as in Bob, 1198A as in Adam, P as in Peter, 6613. General collateral is described on line 13 as office machines. The registering agent is Brown and Black, 312 Water Street, Rainy River, Ontario. The next screen [on the computer terminal] is an amendment, registered on the second of January, 1974, sequence number 1115. The record to be amended is identified as sequence number 1012, and the debtor name is Smith Enterprises. Line 9 is amended. The original line reads: 121 Main Street, Rainy River, Ontario. The amended line reads: 12 King Street, Rainy River, Ontario. The reason given for the amendment is: The secured party address is changed. That's all the information relating to that registration. There are no other registrations.

A PPSA search can reveal everything from small consumer transactions to sales on credit to large-scale corporate financing. It is also of considerable value to anyone purchasing a motor vehicle, because it can warn the buyer if that vehicle has been used for collateral in a registered loan—that is, as a lien against personal property.

Corporations Securities Registration Act Search   In provinces that have both a Personal Property Security Act and a Corporations Securities Registration Act (CSRA), the information you can obtain overlaps. The PPSA gives a brief description of the security agreement, whereas under the CSRA you can pull the actual *instrument* (the legal document that has created a right). The CSRA registers only *corporate* securities, not individual indebtedness.

To do a CSRA search, you must first learn when the corporation was incorporated under a particular name and what length of time it kept the name. This requires at least one corporate search. The next step is to search through the annual Index Books, starting with the year the business was incorporated and working forward to the present. This manual search reveals any registered securities and an instrument number, although the details of the agreement aren't provided.

Once you have this information you must fill out a form, listing the name of the business and the instrument number. This allows you to view the actual instrument. On some forms, to view the Index Books you check off the "search mortgage" category; to see the documents you check off "mortgage instrument."

The CSRA search can be time-consuming if the corporation has changed its name. You must search through the Index Books from the date of incorporation until the name changed, then search through them again from the date it began using the new name. To learn the names, of course, requires separate corporate searches.

In some provinces you may have to go to several departments and find the information under several statutes in order to determine the indebtedness of a corporation. In Nova Scotia, for example, you must do a CSRA search and then look for further records under the Registry of Deeds.

With the exception of the basic corporate search, the kinds of searches described in this chapter apply to provinces other than Quebec. Because of its civil law system, Quebec doesn't have a PPSA, CSRA, or other similar filing system. Still, it is possible to search for one form of indebtedness in Quebec—*trust deeds*. In order to pull these records, one must know where the company's assets are located. They may or may not be kept at the company's head office. To find where the head office is, you can request a straight corporate search over the telephone from the provincial office responsible for companies in Montreal or Quebec City. Then you must search through the Registration Bureau at the local courthouse.

Certificate of Status Search   A certificate of status search varies in cost, depending on whether you want a verbal reply or a certified document. Most provincial offices can tell you if a business has been dissolved or if it has made all the filings required under provincial law and therefore has a valid certificate of status. The name of this document differs slightly from one province to another.

Corporations Tax Branch Search   In some provinces the Ministry of Revenue or corresponding department can tell you if a business has filed up-to-date tax returns. If it hasn't, the company may be in financial trouble.

Workers' Compensation Board Records   By contacting your provincial Workers' Compensation Board, you may be able to find out if a business is in good standing with the department.

Land Registry
Files
_____

Are you thinking of purchasing a house, and you want to find out how much the current owners paid for it? Do you want to trace the land ownership and research any liens and mortgages against a property? You're researching a company and want to see if it has taken out a mortgage on any properties? Or perhaps you want to know if the government has registered the fact that you've paid off your mortgage? All such inquiries can be answered by using provincial land registry files.

First, establish where the land is and which registry office is applicable. You can obtain a list of land registry offices from the Land Registrar in your province. The addresses and names of these registrars are listed in *The Source Book: The Corpus Almanac*, available in any library. The registrars can also advise you how to proceed with your search.

In the following pages I offer some general guidelines on how to search a title. They should *not* be misconstrued as a foolproof method of title searching for the purpose of purchasing land or a house. If you want to certify land ownership, hire a lawyer; however, you can still obtain a lot of information without the help of a lawyer.

A land registry office is a very busy place. At one time most lawyers who specialized in real estate did their own title searching. Today it is done by clerks, often on a piecemeal basis for law firms and other professionals who require information on land ownership. These clerks, as well as the people who run the offices, can be very helpful. Ask them for instructions on how to search the title of your property.

Legal Description   Begin by determining the legal description of the property you are searching. Properties are described differently in each province; the terminology may vary even within a province. In Nova Scotia and Newfoundland they have a Book and Folio Number; in Alberta and British Columbia it is a Parcel Number; in

Manitoba and Saskatchewan it is a Lot and Plan Number. And in Ontario you search for a Lot and Plan Number, a Lot and Concession Number, or possibly a Parcel and Section Number.

Ask the clerk at the Registry Office to see the assessment rolls; they will provide you with the correct legal description.

Land Registry   There are different systems in place for registering land ownership. You may, for example, encounter the centuries-old *Registry System*, which records land ownership in large books known as abstract books. If this is the case, you fill out an abstract slip, providing the legal description of the property, pay a small fee at the cashier, and then you are allowed to see the abstract book.

Under the Registry System you can trace land ownership back as far as you want. Lawyers generally trace ownership back 40 years to ascertain the legal title of the property. This system also uses the words *deed* (or *grant*) and *mortgage* in the abstract book. A deed refers to a change in ownership; a mortgage indicates an encumbrance.

There are different forms of property ownership. One form is joint ownership, meaning that more than one party owns a portion of the property; another type of split ownership is tenants in common. And, of course, one person may own property.

Property can also be owned by a company. If you want to find out who runs the company, you have to do a corporate search, described earlier in this chapter.

The abstract book lists all the appropriate instruments or legal documents. If you want to see an instrument, such as the mortgage, copy down the instrument number and fill out an instrument slip; a nominal fee (usually under $2) is charged. Some of these documents include a Land Transfer Tax Affidavit, which states how much was paid for the property.

Occasionally the purchase price is deliberately left out of the affidavit, because the owner wishes to keep the information confidential. However, the owner pays property taxes to the provincial Ministry of Revenue, or equivalent ministry, at a separate office. The property deed is stamped by the Ministry of Revenue and then registered at the Registry Office, and the receipt number for this transaction is kept at the Registry Office. Take down the receipt number and contact the ministry—you may be able to learn the purchase price this way.

Land Titles   Another method of recording land ownership is the *Land Titles System*. Under this system, with certain exceptions, the provincial government *guarantees* the ownership of the property; this isn't the case under the Registry System. By completing an abstract request slip and paying a small fee, you can obtain a list (also called an abstract)—and which you can keep, by the way—of the most recent owners of, as well as any instruments affecting, the said lands. The term used to indicate ownership under the Land Titles System is *transfer*.

If you want to know if a mortgage on a property has been paid off, check to see if the mortgage (called a *charge* under this system) has been crossed off the list. (The Registry System uses the term *discharge of mortgage* in most provinces. In Ontario, however, mortgages are also crossed out.)

The registry office also lists any liens against a property, such as a *Mechanic's Lien* (sometimes called a *Construction Lien*). If a tradesman has done some work on a property and hasn't been paid, he or she can register a Mechanic's Lien on the property at the registry office and then take legal action against the property owner.

It is also important to know about the *Day Book*. Ten minutes after you have completed a search, a lawyer may come into the registry office and register a change in ownership. It can take a few days before this information is added to the abstract. The Day Book lists any documents that have been filed that day.

The procedures discussed for tracing land ownership generally apply in the province of Quebec. While the actual system of registration is different there than in the rest of the country, you can still pull deeds of sale and mortgages in the same manner. There are 82 land registration offices in Quebec, which are often located in the local courthouse of the town or city closest to the land in question.

Motor Vehicle   Thinking of hiring a chauffeur and need a
Searches   history of a driver's record? Or perhaps you
                    are looking for an old friend, and city directories, tax assessment rolls, and voters' lists at every level of government have failed to give you any leads? In each of these instances, access to various provincial motor vehicle records may supply the information you need.

The public's right of access to these records, however, varies widely from province to province. Ontario appears to be one of the most liberal provinces as far as right of access to this information is concerned. At the time of writing, anyone can conduct a vehicle record search, driver record search, or accident report search in Ontario. The searches involve simply filling in a form.

Motor Vehicle Search   To conduct a motor vehicle search in Ontario, you need the licence plate number of the car you want to research and/or a full name and address. This verifies the name and address of the plate's owner and the make of the car registered in that person's name. (By law, anyone taking up permanent residence in another province must file a change of address within three months.) The motor vehicle search also tells you the ownership of the plate for the current year and the previous three years. This search costs $5.

Driver Record Search   In Ontario you can conduct a driver record search with only a name, although not if the name is a common one, like Smith. Your chances of finding information are enhanced if you have other information that can identify the driver, such as date of birth, driver's licence number, or a middle initial.

This search tells you if the driver has had any convictions under Ontario's Highway Traffic Act or under the Criminal Code of Canada, with respect to driving a vehicle. To learn the actual details of these offences, you have to search through court records; they provide the date of any offences and a list of any suspensions. The cost is $5 per search.

Accident Report Search   Like the other motor vehicle searches, to conduct an accident report search, you must fill out a form providing as much information as possible. This type of search can be done by anyone in Ontario and provides you with a copy of a police accident report. You should be able to provide one party's name in full and the approximate date and place of the accident, or a driver's licence number. The cost is $10 per search.

These searches are currently possible in Ontario. However, with the introduction of a provincial freedom of information bill, and the establishment of the provincial Human Rights Code and federal Charter of Rights, there are growing pressures to curb the dissemination of this information.

Other provinces record the same information provided in the

above searches, but they are far more reluctant to release it. To do any of the above searches in the other provinces, you must submit a written request, giving a detailed explanation why you are requesting the information and how you intend to use it. Each request is carefully monitored to respect individual privacy.

Yet this doesn't mean you can't obtain the information. In British Columbia, for example, if a company wants to hire a driver, it may be able to pull a driver's record if it can convince the provincial authorities that the data is being used for an employee check.

Here's another example: If you want to trace a relative in Nova Scotia and the government finds your request acceptable, it may contact the relative on your behalf and have him or her contact you. On the other hand, the Alberta government doesn't co-operate. It refers you to the police department and says that the police have direct access to its files.

To find out the policy in your province contact the Registrar of Motor Vehicles. (In some provinces the name varies slightly; for example, in British Columbia it is the Superintendent of Motor Vehicles.) Call the hotline number to reach this official.

Provincial Vital
Statistics Offices

There may be an occasion when you need to ascertain whether or not a person has married, had children, died, or changed his or her name. Each province keeps this information at its vital statistics office. Learning this information is not easy—access to it is usually determined on a *policy* basis. This means that each province reviews every request and decides whether the reasons given are valid. If, for example, you need information for a court proceeding, it may be provided. It may also be advantageous to have your lawyer write for you, particularly if you require certified copies of documents rather than a verbal response.

Here is another example: You are a woman living with a man who you suspect is lying about his marital status. You may be able to learn the truth by putting your request in writing and stating your reason. In a case like this, the vital statistics office may tell you if the person has been married and the year of the marriage.

If you are a family member, you stand a better chance of obtaining copies of documents. If you are investigating someone else's background for a valid reason, you can probably obtain only verbal confirmation that an event occurred.

Put your request in writing, providing the reasons why you want the information and how you intend to use it. Provide as much information about the person(s) as possible, including full name and approximate date of marriage or death. Fees vary but are generally under $10 per search. The following is a list of provincial vital statistics offices and whom you can write to there:

Yukon Territory
Mr. Alan Davidson
Registrar, Vital Statistics
Government of Yukon Territory
P. O. Box 2703
Whitehorse, Yukon
Y1A 2C6
Telephone: (403) 667-5811

Northwest Territories
Mrs. Rita Matheson
Deputy Registrar General
Government of Northwest Territories
P. O. Box 1320
Yellowknife, Northwest Territories
X1A 2L9
Telephone: (403) 873-7210

British Columbia
Mr. A. H. Hersom, Director
Division of Vital Statistics
Department of Health Services and Hospital Insurance
1515 Blanshard Street
Parliament Buildings
Victoria, British Columbia
V8V 1X4
Telephone: (604) 386-3166

Alberta
Mr. S. W. Gilroy
Director of Vital Statistics
Department of Health and Social Development
10405–100 Avenue
Edmonton, Alberta

T5J 0A6
Telephone: (403) 427-2681

Saskatchewan
Mrs. V. Cloarex
Director of Vital Statistics
T. C. Douglas Building
3475 Albert Street
Regina, Saskatchewan
S4S 6X6
Telephone: (306) 565-3092

Manitoba
Ms. Marjories Kreton
Division of Vital Statistics
Department of Health and Social Development
Room 104, Norquay Building
Winnipeg, Manitoba
R3C 0V8
Telephone: (204) 944-4168

Ontario
Mrs. R. E. Drapkin
Deputy Registrar General
Macdonald Block
Parliament Buildings
Toronto, Ontario
M7A 1Y5
Telephone: (416) 965-2274

Quebec
M. Lorenzo Servant
Responsable des archives civiles
Ministère de la justice
Registre de référence
117 rue St-André
Québec, Québec
G1K 3Y3
Telephone: (418) 643-6436

New Brunswick
Ms. Marianne Wiezel
Acting Registrar General
Vital Statistics Division
Department of Health
P. O. Box 6000
Fredericton, New Brunswick
E3B 5H1
Telephone: (506) 453-2717

Nova Scotia
Mr. D. F. Arthur
Deputy Registrar General
Department of Public Health
Halifax, Nova Scotia
B3J 2M9
Telephone: (902) 424-4374

Prince Edward Island
Ms. G. A. Melanson, Director
Division of Vital Statistics
P. O. Box 2000
Charlottetown, Prince Edward Island
C1A 7N8
Telephone: (902) 892-5471

Newfoundland
Mr. Norman M. Parker, Registrar
Vital Statistics Division
Department of Health
St. John's, Newfoundland
A1C 5T7
Telephone: (709) 737-3310

Provincial
Freedom of
Information
Laws
_____

Provincial freedom of information laws are a good source for finding out what sort of information the government keeps on you and whether or not it is accurate. Most provinces are now moving to enact freedom of information laws. These laws have different names, but the principle involved in each of them is the same: that citizens have the legal right to see government information about themselves.

New Brunswick, Nova Scotia (which in 1977 became the first province to offer such legislation), Newfoundland, and Quebec have proclaimed freedom of information laws. Most of the other provinces are now at various stages of enacting such legislation.

Generally speaking, this legislation allows you to access many government files with information on you. But it also provides many exceptions, including denying any access to information that may hinder any investigatory proceedings and that may invade another person's privacy.

If the information you seek is denied, you can appeal; however, the appeal process varies considerably from province to province. For example, in Nova Scotia there is no provision to appeal a denial of information to the courts. But in New Brunswick you can refer the matter to either the provincial ombudsman or a judge of the Supreme Court.

The actual mechanics of retrieving personal information under freedom of information legislation also varies. To find out if there is a bill in effect in your province and what it provides, contact the government bookstore or visit the government section of your local library. You can also contact the department responsible for administering the law. If all of these leads fail, call the provincial hotline number given earlier in this chapter.

If there is no freedom of information law in effect in your province, you may still have access to information on yourself. To learn what sort of information is available, contact the individual or department involved in drafting this legislation. When the Ontario government was preparing its legislation, the Minister without Portfolio, Norman W. Sterling, compiled the *Index of Personal Information Systems*. This guide describes every provincial government file on Ontario residents, and many of the hundreds of information banks listed are available to individuals who want information on *themselves*. The guide is 215 pages long, was published in 1981, and is available free of charge from:

Provincial Secretariat for Resources Development
Room 1620
Whitney Block
Toronto, Ontario
M7A 1A2
Telephone: (416) 965-9499

Ontario is the only province I know of that has this type of index. In provinces without a freedom of information bill, you may have to contact every department to find out what files are kept and how to access them.

Accessing Federal
Government Sources
Chapter Seventeen

With over half a million employees on its payroll, the Government of Canada is the country's largest custodian of information. Many civil servants with expertise in virtually every field are available to help you solve your information needs. Take advantage of their knowledge—after all, as a taxpayer, you're paying for it!

The jurisdictions of the federal government are wide-ranging. Set out in Section 91 of the Constitution Act, 1867, they cover everything from unemployment insurance to defence.

There are two fundamental divisions within the federal government: *departments* (including ministries and Crown corporations, all of which are structured differently and have various functions) and *commissions*, *boards*, and *councils* (independent of departments). Most of our information needs are supplied by departments.

Locating
Departments
and Civil
Servants

The challenge of finding federal government sources is zeroing in on the appropriate department and, eventually, the most knowledgeable civil servant. To help you, the federal government has established the *Centre for Service to the Public*, which in turn operates several *Canada Service Bureaus* across the country. Operating under the jurisdiction of the Department of Supply and Services, these bureaus are staffed by professionals who refer telephone callers to the appropriate government office. The service is available by telephone only. If you cannot obtain information from a local government department because the data is available only from a department outside the city, the staff at the local Canada Service Bureau can connect you, wherever you are in Canada, to the long-distance number—*free of charge*—or have the department call you directly. Keep this in mind for any federal government number given in this chapter. It means that if you can't obtain the information you need locally, you never have to place a long-distance telephone call to find it. Not only that: If there isn't a Canada Service Bureau in your town or city, you can call the nearest one *toll-free*.

Bureau staff can help you obtain copies of reports, explain your eligibility for a grant, or refer you to the most suitable civil servant. Be patient if you don't find the right person immediately—it may take a few conversations. The following is a list of Canada Service Bureaus, including their local and toll-free telephone numbers:*

Yukon Territory
Yukon Inquiry Service (operated jointly with the territory)
Telephone: In Whitehorse: 667-5811
In other parts of the Yukon (toll-free): Zenith 3003

British Columbia
Canada Service Bureau
Telephone: In Vancouver: 666-5555
In northern British Columbia (toll-free): Zenith 08918
In other parts of the province: 112-800-663-1381

Alberta
Canada Service Bureau
Telephone: In Edmonton: 420-2021
In Calgary: 231-4998
In other parts of the province (toll-free): 1-800-232-9481

Saskatchewan
Canada Service Bureau
Telephone: In Regina: 359-6683
In other parts of the province (toll-free): Zenith 28000

---

*For hours of operation, call your local Canada Service Bureau.

Manitoba
Canada Service Bureau
Telephone: In Winnipeg: 945-3744 (answered by Manitoba Citizens'
            Inquiry service, operated through a joint federal-
            provincial agreement)
            In other parts of the province (toll-free): 1-800-282-8060

Ontario
Canada Service Bureau
Telephone: In Toronto: 926-1993
            In Ottawa: 995-7151
            In North Bay: 476-4910
            In area codes 807 and 705 (toll-free): 1-800-461-1664
            In other parts of the province (toll-free): 1-800-268-7207

Quebec
Canada Service Bureau
Telephone: In Montreal: 283-3333
            In Quebec City: 694-7738
            In other parts of the province (toll-free): 1-800-361-7287

New Brunswick
Canada Service Bureau
Telephone: In Moncton: 388-6030 (answered by New Brunswick
            Citizens' Inquiry service, operated through a joint
            federal-provincial agreement)
            In other parts of the province (toll-free): 1-800-442-4400

Nova Scotia
Canada Service Bureau
Telephone: In Halifax: 426-8092
            In other parts of the province (toll-free): 1-426-8092

Prince Edward Island
Island Inquiries (operated jointly with the province)
Telephone: In Charlottetown: 566-7575
            In other parts of the province (toll-free): 1-566-7575

Newfoundland
Canada Service Bureau
Telephone: In St. John's: 772-4365
            In other parts of the province (toll-free): Zenith 07027

An excellent reference source, and one the staff at the bureaus use themselves, is the *Index to Federal Programs and Services*. This annual reference book, which is available at most libraries, lists 1,200 federal programs and services with a brief description of each, 4,500 addresses, regular telephone numbers and toll-free numbers of many departments, and a subject index. If you plan to use federal government sources on a regular basis, it's worth purchasing a copy of this book ($9.95) from any bookstore authorized to act as an agent for the federal government. (Bookstore agents are discussed later in this chapter.)

The federal government publishes detailed telephone directories for every province, including one for the Ottawa region. In addition, Southam Communications publishes the very useful *Corpus Administrative Index*. With a separate supplementary subject guide, it lists all federal and provincial government departments, key personnel, addresses, and telephone numbers. Similar directories include *The Source Book: The Corpus Almanac* and the *Canadian Almanac and Directory*. These can all be found in most libraries.

Locating Federal Government Publications

There are various ways in which you can search for a federal government publication:

- You can telephone a Canada Service Bureau for assistance.
- You can search through the *Microlog Index* at the public library. (For a description of this index, refer to Chapter 14, "Using Libraries in Canada," and Chapter 16, "Accessing Provincial Government Sources.")
- If you're searching for a monograph (material that is not a periodical, magazine, or bulletin), you can refer to the federal government's *Government of Canada Publications Quarterly Catalogue* and *Weekly Checklist of Canadian Government Publications*. There is also the *Special List of Canadian Government Publications*, which highlights major publications, and the *Subject List*, which lists publications by subject. All of these guides are pub-

lished by Canada's official government publisher, the Canadian Government Publishing Centre, a division of the Department of Supply and Services. These lists are often available at the government publications section of large public libraries.

The Canadian Government Publishing Centre has a backlist of over 10,000 monographs, and most of these can be found in public depository libraries across Canada. To obtain a free list of these depositories, call the Publishing Centre at (819) 997-2560 and ask them to mail you a copy of the pamphlet, "Where and How to Obtain Canadian Government Publications."

Authorized bookstore agents sell these monographs, too. For a list of agents, contact the Publishing Centre and ask for a copy of their free brochure, "Authorized Bookstore Agents for the Sale of Canadian Government Publications." The agents sell most major titles and have all the guides mentioned above, as well as a list of all previously published titles.

You can also normally find what you need in the public library, or you can order the publication directly from the department that compiled the material. If you are still unsuccessful, you can often purchase a copy of the publication from Micromedia Limited, Toronto.

• In addition to publications that you have to purchase, there are also publications that are distributed *free of charge*. Each department has its own mailing list of people who receive these publications. For a list of federal departments, their addresses, and telephone numbers, call the Canadian Government Publishing Centre and request a copy of their pamphlet, "Government of Canada Information Services Free Publications," then call the appropriate department and ask to be placed on its mailing list.

You can also use the contacts in this pamphlet to inquire about published materials other than monographs, such as limited distribution reports (described in Chapter 16, "Accessing Provincial Government Sources"). For example, the *New Products Bulletin* can be of tremendous benefit to investors in the manufacturing industry. It is published on an irregular basis by the Department of Regional Industrial Expansion "to inform Canadian industry of licensing and joint venture opportunities that may be investigated for the purpose of forming manufacturing affiliations." Anyone in the industry can obtain a free subscription by telephoning (613) 995-2235.

If, for example, you are interested in finding out which companies have received grants from the Department of Supply and Services, you can refer to the *Bulletin of Business Opportunities,* published on a weekly basis. It's available free of charge by telephoning (819) 997-7363. Or say you want to know the amount of donations made to any of the three federal political parties and who made them: Refer to the *Registered Party Fiscal Period Returns,* published by the Chief Electoral Officer (an *agency* of Parliament, not a department). A copy of this annual publication costs $12. For further information, you can telephone the office directly at (613) 993-2975.

Keeping
Informed about
Government
Business

The most popular way to keep informed about what is happening at the federal government level is by reading *Hansard*, the official transcript of all House of Commons proceedings. *Hansard*, plus a subject and personal name index, are kept at public libraries. You can purchase copies from government bookstore agents or directly from the Canadian Government Publishing Centre. (A similar service is available for the proceedings of the Senate.)

Another method of keeping informed about federal government business, and regulations affecting private business, is by referring to the weekly publication *Canada Gazette, Part One*. (Part Two of this publication lists all new government regulations, along with details of new federal acts, and appears every second week. Part Three, published irregularly, lists all new acts immediately after they have received royal assent.)

The *Ottawa Letter* is another good source of federal government information. It describes the activities of the executive, judicial, and legislative branches. Available at most libraries, it is published weekly in a loose-leaf format.

A similar service is *Canadian News Facts*, which provides a synopsis of important news items, including federal government news. It is also published on a weekly basis in a loose-leaf form by Marpep Publishing; it, too, can be found in most libraries.

It is impossible in a book of this scope to provide more than a mere sampling of departmental sources at the federal government level. As is the case with provincial government sources, I have highlighted a few federal sources that have assisted me in my research. If you follow the guidelines presented at the beginning of this chapter, you should be able to tap additional sources as well.

Department of Consumer and Corporate Affairs	You may require information on the legal status of a corporation because you're planning to lend it money, or perhaps you've just inherited some shares from a relative's estate.

You may also need to verify if a trademark has been registered or to examine or obtain copies of a balance sheet showing reported revenues, assets, and earnings of a public or private federally registered corporation. You can acquire all this information over the telephone free of charge. Here's how:

Corporations Branch   *All* federal corporations must file at least three forms in order to be incorporated under the Canada Business Corporations Act: Form 1: Articles of Incorporation, Form 3: Notice of Registered Office, and Form 6: Notice of Directors. They are reproduced in Table 17.1. The information recorded on them can be obtained over the telephone by dialing the inquiries unit at (819) 997-1142. You can obtain copies of up to nine documents free of charge and have these mailed to you by calling the photocopying area of the Corporations Branch at (819) 997-3462.

Federal corporations must comply with other filing requirements, too. All distributing (public) corporations, and all non-distributing (private) corporations with assets of $5 million or revenues over $10 million, must file an annual, audited financial statement. The Corporations Branch has between 5,000 and 6,000 of these financial statements on file, and although this number is small in comparison to the over 120,000 federal corporations active in Canada, it does represent the most significant ones. A financial statement includes information on gross revenues, assets, net earnings, and other financial details and is considered one document. It can be mailed to you, or specific figures from it can be disclosed over the telephone. You can also find out, by telephone, whether the annual returns, any changes of directors, or any changes of registered offices have been filed.

In a few rare instances, a corporation that is required to file a financial statement may obtain an exemption if it can prove to the Director of the Corporations Branch that the information may be detrimental to its business interests.

TABLE 17.1 Form 1: Articles of Incorporation

CANADA BUSINESS CORPORATIONS ACT	▮✦▮	LOI SUR LES SOCIÉTÉS COMMERCIALES CANADIENNES
FORM 1		FORMULE 1
ARTICLES OF INCORPORATION (SECTION 6)		STATUTS CONSTITUTIFS (ARTICLE 6)

1 – Name of Corporation   Dénomination de la société

2 – The place in Canada where the registered office is to be situated   Lieu au Canada ou doit être situé le siège social

3 – The classes and any maximum number of shares that the corporation is authorized to issue   Catégories et tout nombre maximal d'actions que la société est autorisée à émettre

4 – Restrictions if any on share transfers   Restrictions sur le transfert des actions s'il y a lieu

5 – Number (or minimum and maximum number) of directors   Nombre (ou nombre minimum et maximum) d'administrateurs

6 – Restrictions if any on business the corporation may carry on   Limites imposées quant aux activités commerciales que la société peut exploiter s'il y a lieu

7 – Other provisions if any   Autres dispositions s'il y a lieu

8 – Incorporators   Fondateurs

Names – Noms	Address (include postal code) Adresse (inclure le code postal)	Signature

FOR DEPARTMENTAL USE ONLY   AU USAGE DU MINISTÈRE SEULEMENT

Corporation No – No de la société   Filed   Deposée

CCA 1385 3 81

TABLE 17.1, cont'd   Form 3: Notice of Registered Office

<table>
<tr>
<td colspan="2">
**CANADA BUSINESS
CORPORATIONS ACT**

FORM 3
NOTICE OF REGISTERED OFFICE OR
NOTICE OF CHANGE OF REGISTERED OFFICE
</td>
<td>[flag]</td>
<td>
**LOI SUR LES SOCIÉTÉS
COMMERCIALES CANADIENNES**

FORMULE 3
AVIS DU LIEU DU SIÈGE SOCIAL
OU AVIS DE CHANGEMENT DE LIEU DU SIÈGE SOCIAL
</td>
</tr>
<tr>
<td colspan="3">1 — Name of Corporation — Dénomination de la société</td>
<td>2 — Corporation No. — No. de la société</td>
</tr>
<tr>
<td colspan="4">3 — Address of the registered office   Adresse du siège social</td>
</tr>
<tr>
<td colspan="4">4 — Effective date of change   Date effective du changement</td>
</tr>
<tr>
<td colspan="4">5 — Previous address of the registered office   Adresse précédente du siège social</td>
</tr>
<tr>
<td>Date</td>
<td>Signature</td>
<td colspan="2">Description of Office — Description du poste</td>
</tr>
<tr>
<td colspan="4">CCA-1386 (1-83)</td>
</tr>
</table>

TABLE 17.1, cont'd   Form 6: Notice of Directors

CANADA BUSINESS CORPORATIONS ACT	LOI SUR LES SOCIÉTÉS COMMERCIALES CANADIENNES
FORM 6	FORMULE 6
NOTICE OF DIRECTORS OR NOTICE OF CHANGE OF DIRECTORS	AVIS DES ADMINISTRATEURS OU AVIS DE CHANGEMENT DES ADMINISTRATEURS

1 – Name of Corporation – Dénomination de la société

2 – Corporation No. – N° de la société

3 – The following persons became directors of this corporation   Les personnes suivantes sont devenues administrateurs de la présente société

Effective Date – Date d'entrée en vigueur

Name – Nom	Residental Address – Adresse résidentielle	Occupation	Resident Canadian Résident canadien

4 – The following persons ceased to be directors of this corporation   Les personnes suivantes ont cessé d'être administrateurs de la présente société

Effective Date – Date d'entrée en vigueur

Name – Nom	Residental Address – Adresse résidentielle

5 – The directors of this corporation now are   Les administrateurs de la présente société sont maintenant

Name – Nom	Residental Address – Adresse résidentielle	Occupation	Resident Canadian Résident canadien

Date	Signature	Description of Office – Description du poste

CCA-1388 (4-79)

If one corporation amalgamates with another, it must file Form 9: Articles of Amalgamation. If it changes its corporate name, it must file Form 4: Articles of Amendment, along with the appropriate name-search report. There are over 15 different forms that federally incorporated companies may be required to file; however, Forms 1, 3, and 6 contain the information that all these businesses must file and that you can access most easily.

The Corporations Branch maintains computer records on 120,000 active federal corporations. In addition, it keeps track of 2,500,000 provincially incorporated companies and trademark records using a computer system called NUANS. The Branch is now encouraging provincial authorities to provide machine-readable tapes of all provincially registered sole proprietorships and partnerships for inclusion in the NUANS data base. At the time of writing, it had incorporated these files for the provinces of Ontario and Manitoba. Therefore, by telephoning the Branch and providing merely the name of a business, you can learn when the company began, whether or not it is federally or provincially incorporated or otherwise, and where to find the information you need.

Trade Marks Branch   If you want to find out who has registered a trademark or design for a product, telephone the Trade Marks Branch at (819) 997-1420. The staff will tell you the owner of the trademark, the company's name and address, and when any one of the more than 200,000 trademarks was registered with the Department of Consumer and Corporate Affairs. You can also ask for the name of the agent or representative of the owner of the trademark and any associated trademarks. There is no charge for a verbal reply; however, if you require photocopies of documents, you must visit the Trade Marks Branch in Hull, Quebec.

Bankruptcy Branch   There are several ways to find out whether a business or an individual has gone into voluntary bankruptcy. For a quick, verbal verification, telephone the Bankruptcy Branch at (819) 997-2053. This is where all bankruptcies are registered, but only basic information, such as where it took place and the monies involved, is kept on file.

The full files of a bankruptcy proceeding are kept at any one of the 14 local District Insolvency Offices, as well as at the Supreme Court of each province. The major documents include: a list of the assets, liabilities, and dividends involved; Assignment of Bankruptcy forms; the Statement of Affairs; a Certificate of Appointment of Trustees; the notes of examination under oath (if an examination has been conducted); the minutes of the first meeting of creditors; and the trustees' Statement of Receipts and Disbursements.

The local District Insolvency Office keeps the *originals* of these documents for three weeks after the first meeting of creditors, then sends them to the Supreme Court of the province. It keeps a *copy* of the documents for one year after the trustees' discharge, after which time they are sent to its archives. You can therefore visit the District Insolvency Office and inspect the original documents if the bankruptcy is recent. If it isn't, you can do a court record search.

Bureau of Competitive Policy   The Marketing Practices branch of the Bureau of Competitive Policy publishes a useful quarterly publication, *Misleading Advertising Bulletin*. The bulletin provides a list of all convictions under the misleading advertising and deceptive marketing practices provisions of the Combines and Investigation Act and lists the name of the accused, the location of the offence, and the disposition. You can then follow up any case by accessing the full court record. The bulletin is available at some of the larger public libraries and at most law libraries.

Statistics Canada   Statistics Canada, on behalf of the federal government, works with every aspect of statistical information. The department publishes a broad range of materials, and no matter what your topic, there is usually an expert statistician who can either provide you with the information you need or give you advice on how to get it.

For example, a CBC producer once hired me to investigate the moving business in Canada. Among other things, she wanted to know how many people moved each year. This wasn't as easy a question to answer as it seemed. However, as you can see in Table 17.2, the staff at Statistics Canada made a sincere effort to gather data for me and actually came up with more detailed information than I was originally seeking. This demonstrates the extent of the information you can gather by contacting the right civil servant.

Most of the staff at this department is based in Ottawa, although there are Statistics Canada offices located across the country. An extremely useful guide for finding the best experts is the *Data Users Directory: Who to Dial at Statistics Canada*. You can order a free

TABLE 17.2   Information Obtained from Statistics Canada

Statistics   Statistique
Canada   Canada

Ottawa, Canada

K1A OT6

February 6, 1984

Mr. Steve Overbury,
"Market Place",
Canadian Broadcasting Corporation,

Toronto, Ontario
M4P 2A4

Dear Mr. Overbury:

You will find attached a document summarizing the situation of the household goods moving activity between 1973 and 1980. It has to be understood that the For-hire Trucking Survey from which these estimates have been produced covers only the non-local movement (more than 25 kilometres) of companies that had earned $100,000 or more of intercity transportation revenue during the preceding year. Therefore, the figures presented in the attached table underestimate the total measure of the activity. We do not think, however, that this situation should significantly affect the interpretation of the statistics. For a detailed description of the For-hire Trucking Survey, its coverage and methodology please consult the publication "For-hire Trucking Survey" (Catalogue 53-224) Furthermore, please note that the attached table refers only to the inter-provincial movement of household goods (i.e. intra-provincial movement has been excluded).

If you need further assistance, or if you have any questions do not hesitate to call Mr. Steven Mozes or Mr. Yvan Deslauriers at 1-613-995-1976.

Yours truly,

Barbara Slater

Barbara J. Slater,
Director,
Transportation and Communications Division

Att.

Canadä

Summary Statistics on the Inter-provincial, Inter-territorial and Territorial/Provincial Transportation of Used Household Goods within Canada

Year	Interprovincial, Inter-territorial and Territorial/Provincial Transportation of Used Household Goods by All Carriers		Interprovincial, Inter-Territorial and Territorial/Provincial Transportation of Used Household Goods by Van Line Affiliates		The Percentage of Interprovincial, Inter-territorial and Territorial/Provincial Transportation of Used Household Goods by Van Line Affiliates to All Carriers	
	Estimated ($) Revenues	CV(%)	Estimated ($) Revenues	CV(%)	Estimated (MS%) Market Share	CV(%)
1973	39,727,000	16.22	35,806,000	14.12	90.13	1.06
1974	42,928,000	4.77	37,642,000	0.48	87.69	2.15
1975	52,795,000	3.88	49,445,000	0.43	93.66	1.73
1976	69,590,000	1.09	65,144,000	4.35	93.61	1.63
1977	82,006,000	9.35	77,050,000	8.77	93.96	0.30
1978	87,978,000	1.81	84,036,000	0.62	95.52	0.59
1979	104,244,000	3.10	91,762,000	0.48	88.04	1.80
1980	111,562,000	4.01	102,907,000	0.59	92.24	2.30

MS: Market Share

CV: Coefficient of Variation

Note: This table is compiled from the annual For-hire Trucking Survey (Catalogue 53-224) and relates to the sector of the Motor Carrier Transportation Industry dealing with the inter-provincial, inter-territorial and territorial/provincial transportation of used household goods within Canada.

copy by calling your local Statistics Canada office. If there isn't an office near you, call one of the numbers listed below, toll-free:

- Yukon and Northern British Columbia (area served by NorwesTel Inc.): Zenith 08913.
- Northwest Territories: Zenith 22015.
- British Columbia (area served by B.C. Tel): 112-800-663-1551.
- Alberta: 1-800-222-6400.
- Saskatchewan: 1 (112) 800-667-3524.
- Manitoba: 1-800-282-8006.
- Ontario: 1-800-268-1151.
- Quebec: 1-800-361-2831.
- Nova Scotia, New Brunswick, and Prince Edward Island: 1-800-565-7192.
- Newfoundland and Labrador: Zenith 07037.

You can also call these numbers and ask for the department's publications list. Some of the booklets, such as *Answers to Questions on Labour Statistics, A Union Guide,* can help you interpret statistics.

If you require information on the corporate structure of Canadian society, one of the best sources is a publication by Statistics Canada called *Inter-Corporate Ownership.* This is a fat reference book available at most libraries that provides a detailed list of businesses in Canada, their subsidiaries, and the degree of any foreign ownership. It also includes information from the federal government's Corporations and Labour Unions Returns Act, the *Canada Gazette,* the Foreign Investment Review Act, newspaper and magazine articles, Moody's, Standard and Poor's, Jane's, and *Who Owns Whom.* At the time of writing, the latest edition of *Inter-Corporate Ownership* was published in 1982, with a revised edition planned for 1986.

The information contained in this publication is regularly updated on computer. If you are using the 1982 edition and require a single update, you can call Statistics Canada at (819) 990-9858 and ask for the information. The department does not update entries on a regular basis but does honour the occasional request; if you need updated information on a number of companies, there is a hefty charge. If you require up-to-date information regularly, it would be wise to subscribe to the Canada Systems Group's "Inter-Corporate Ownership" data base, available in Canada from the Info Globe computer service.

Department of
Finance
A useful source for finding out the indebtedness of a company or of individuals involved in a company, is the Bank of Canada's registrations system. A provision under Section 178 of the federal Bank Act governs certain categories of loans made by any Canadian chartered bank to companies involved in various kinds of manufacturing, farming, fishing, and so forth. A chartered bank making a loan under Section 178 registers the information at one of the Bank's "agency point" offices.

You can conduct a search in person or mail in your request, along with $2 per name, at any one of these offices, by merely supplying a name. The offices are located in Vancouver (for all of British Columbia, the Northwest Territories, and the Yukon), Calgary, Regina, Winnipeg, Toronto, Montreal, Halifax, and Saint John (for New Brunswick, Newfoundland, and Prince Edward Island).

You are then given the name of the business, the name of the owner, and the name and address of the chartered bank. Information on the amount of the loan or the branch of the bank is not available—to obtain it, you must contact the business directly. This information can alert you to the fact that some of the assets of a business are tied up in a loan.

Labour Canada
If you are an employer or a representative of a union and need information relating to industrial relations or collective bargaining, you should be aware that there is a centralized information clearing house whose services are available to you—the Industrial Relations Information Service (IRIS).

At one time union and management officials relied on several different agencies, such as Statistics Canada, the Economic Council of Canada, the Conference Board of Canada, and the C. D. Howe Institute, to meet their information needs. But with the introduction of IRIS in 1981, anyone in this field can now tap one source that assembles information from many other sources, including Labour Canada's massive library.

You can call IRIS *collect* at (819) 997-3117. The kinds of information IRIS can supply are diverse. For example, if someone requires information on collective bargaining agreements, IRIS can isolate and analyze any of 150 provisions contained in its contract settlement data bank. IRIS stores 10,000 federal agreements and most provincial agreements where 100 or more employees are involved.

IRIS can also provide up-to-date federal and provincial labour-related legislation, arbitration decisions, corporate information, and other data.

IRIS operates with five full-time industrial relations consultants, each responsible for a different region in Canada. In some instances you may be able to access information over the telephone. IRIS can also mail you copies of agreements or, if your need warrants it, arrange an overnight courier service.

IRIS also publishes *Collective Bargaining Information Sources*, a massive, loose-leaf book listing over 400 publications and services of use to anyone involved in industrial relations or collective bargaining. It is available free of charge, and regularly updated sections are mailed out to subscribers, also without cost.

All queries to IRIS are kept strictly confidential.

Public Archives
of Canada

If you're researching *any* aspect of Canadian life, don't overlook the vast amounts of publicly accessible resources at the Public Archives of Canada. Located at 395 Wellington Street, Ottawa, the archives stores an endless array of Canadian and foreign material, including, as a promotional brochure states: "letters, accounts, telegrams, registers, reports, maps, globes, atlases, architectural plans, photographs, watercolours, engravings, sketches and drawings, oil paintings, computer tapes, sound recordings, films, and videocassettes."

The archives are of special interest to anyone tracing their family history. The Manuscript Division of the archives issues a free publication, *Tracing Your Ancestors in Canada*, and you can order a copy by telephoning (613) 995-5138.

Freedom of
Information
Laws

On July 4, 1984 the Canadian Parliament enacted two significant pieces of legislation— the *Access to Information Act* and a related statute, the *Privacy Act*. As is the case with many other laws in this country, Canada followed in the footsteps of other nations, in particular the United States, which passed a Freedom of Information Act in 1966. It is still too early to assess the effectiveness of the Canadian legislation in releasing information to the public.

Privacy Act   Before the Privacy Act was passed, Canadians had some access to the files the federal government kept on them, and some protection over who had access to the information, under Part Four of the Canadian Human Rights Act (which has been in effect since March 1, 1978). The Privacy Act expands the access to, and protection of, personal information on individuals that previously existed.

You can obtain copies of, or examine, any personal information on yourself collected for a federal government program or operation. (There are, of course, certain exemptions, such as any information pertaining to national security or law enforcement agencies.) If there is an error in the information, you may have it corrected by contacting the department that collected it.

Begin by visiting any large public library or post office, and obtain the brochure describing the service and how to use it, "Treasury Board of Canada, Privacy Act." You can also pick up a simple application form, which is reproduced in Table 17.3, and the *Personal Information Index*, which provides a detailed breakdown of most federal government departments and agencies, with a list of the types of information each collects. You must single out the department and sub-department in order to identify the information you require and where it is kept.

No processing fee is charged for providing this information. The federal government is legally bound to reply to your request within 30 days of receiving your application, although it can extend this time limit for an additional 30 days or more for a variety of reasons.

Access to Information Act   This statute, for the first time in Canadian legal history, gives Canadian citizens and permanent residents the legal right to examine, or obtain copies of, records of federal government institutions. Again, the exceptions to this involve anything relating to national security or trade secrets.

To obtain information, visit any large library or post office and read the pamphlet, "Treasury Board of Canada, Access to Information Act." Beside the pamphlets is a simple application form (reproduced in Table 17.4) and the *Access Registry*, which provides an organizational outline of the federal government and details of the information banks of each department or agency.

As with the Privacy Act, you should spend some time reading the *Access Registry* to identify the information bank that stores the information you require. The *Registry* also lists the names and

TABLE 17.3 Sample Personal Information Request Form

Government Gouvernement
of Canada du Canada

Privacy Act

Personal Information Request Form

For official use only

Individuals are required to use this form to request access to personal information about themselves under the Privacy Act.

STEP 1: *Decide whether or not you wish to submit a request under the Privacy Act.* You may decide to request the information informally, without using the procedures required by the Act, through the local office of the appropriate government institution or through the Privacy Co-ordinator listed in the Index of Personal Information. Copies of the Index are available in public libraries, post offices in rural areas and government information offices.

STEP 2: *Consult the Index of Personal Information.* If you have decided to exercise your rights of access under the Privacy Act, review the descriptions of personal information for institutions which are most likely to have the information you are seeking. If you cannot identify the institution, you may seek the advice of the Privacy Commissioner at the address shown in the Index. Decide on the personal information bank or class of personal information likely to contain the information.

STEP 3: *Complete this personal information request form.* Indicate the personal information bank or class of personal information to which you are requesting access, and include any additional information indicated in the bank description to locate the information you are seeking, or to verify your own identity. Indicate whether you wish to receive copies of the information, examine the original in a government office, or if you are requesting other arrangements for access. There is no application fee for making a request under the Privacy Act.

STEP 4: *Send the request to the person identified in the Index* as the appropriate officer responsible for the particular personal information bank or class.

STEP 5: *Review the information you received in response to your request.* Decide if you wish to make further requests under the Privacy Act. You may wish to exercise your rights to request corrections or to require that notations be attached to the information when corrections are not made. You may also decide to complain to the Privacy Commissioner when you believe that you have been denied any of your rights under the Act.

Federal Government Institution

Registration Number and Personal Information Bank or Class of Personal Information

---

I wish to examine the Information ☐ As it is   ☐ All in English   ☐ All in French

Provide other details specified in the Index to aid in locating particular information or to verify identity of applicant. (Present or former members of the Canadian Armed Forces requesting military records must provide additional information as specified in the D.N.D. section of the Index.)

Method of access preferred
☐ Receive copies of the original   ☐ Examine original in government office   ☐ Other method (please specify)

Identification of applicant

Name (or previous name) | Social Insurance No. (or other identifying no. if applicable)

Street address, apartment | City or town

Province, territory, or other | Postal Code | Telephone number(s)

If this request follows a previous enquiry, quote reference number ▶

I have a right to access to personal information about myself under the Privacy Act by virtue of my status as a Canadian citizen, a permanent resident within the meaning of the Immigration Act, 1976, or by Order of the Governor in Council pursuant to subsection 12(3) of the Privacy Act.

_____ Signature   _____ Date

Canada

Français au verso   TBC 350-58 (83/2)

TABLE 17.4   Sample Access to Information Request Form

<table>
<tr><td>■✦ Government
of Canada</td><td>Gouvernement
du Canada</td><td>For official use only</td></tr>
</table>

Access to Information Act

Access to Information Request Form

This form is required to request *records* under the Access to Information Act. Requests for federal government *information* can ordinarily be made by means of a telephone call, a visit, or a written request to the appropriate government information office.

STEP 1: *Decide exactly what information you want* — You can facilitate the search for records and reduce fees by defining as narrowly as you can the particular records you are looking for.

STEP 2: *Consult the Access Register* — The Register contains descriptions of government records, their probable location and other information which will likely assist you in identifying the particular records you wish to see. A copy of the Access Register is available at major libraries, post offices, and government information offices.

STEP 3: *Ask for assistance if necessary* — If you are unable to identify the records you are looking for in the Access Register, contact the Access Co-ordinator of the appropriate department, either in person, by telephone or by letter at the address shown in the Register. The Co-ordinator will assist you in identifying the records.

STEP 4: *Complete this Request Form*, providing as many specific details as you can about the desired records, such as:
— subject, title, author and date;
— specific events, activities, individuals, corporations, products, reports, meetings, decisions, agreements, etc., of interest in the records;
— the number and title of the appropriate class of records, as listed in the Access Register.

STEP 5: *Send in the completed Request Form* with an application fee of $5.00, payable by money order or cheque to the Receiver General of Canada, to the appropriate officer identified in the Access Register. Unless you have already indicated what you are willing to pay for, you will be asked to authorize any fees that may be charged before the work is completed.

Federal Government Institution

Description of Record and Subject Topic of Interest (see step 4)

Class of record, number and title (consult Access Register — see step 2)

Method of access preferred

☐ Receive copies of the original   ☐ Examine original in government office   ☐ Other method (please specify)

Identification of applicant
Name

Street address, apartment   City or town

Province, territory or other   Postal Code   Telephone number(s)

I have a right of access to government records under the Access to Information Act by virtue of my status as a Canadian citizen, a permanent resident within the meaning of the Immigration Act, 1976, or by Order of the Governor in Council pursuant to subsection 4(2) of the Access to Information Act.

Signature   Date

Canada   Français au verso   TBC 350-57 (83/2)

addresses of *access officers* who will be handling your request. To speed up your application, which can take over 80 days to process, *telephone* the access officer—before you send in your application—to make sure you have listed the proper descriptive information. The access officer can help you complete the form and tell you how long it will take to process, as well as your chances of obtaining the information. This initial discussion can also give you an idea of the approximate volume of material you are requesting. Because there is a $5 fee to read your application, an additional $10-per-hour charge for requests that involve over five hours of research, along with further charges for photocopying the material, an estimate at this stage is very helpful.

Canada's freedom of information laws are also designed to safeguard some information, so you may encounter situations where you cannot obtain the information you want. For example, I once requested a copy of a confidential clinical study on a hair restorer lotion called "MJS." This lotion was registered with the Department of Health and Welfare as a drug. I knew that for it to be registered as such with this department, a clinical study proving its effectiveness had had to be submitted, and I wanted to determine how thorough the study was. The access officer told me the study was commercial information of a confidential nature, and he would therefore have to contact the manufacturer of the lotion for permission to release it. I eventually obtained a copy of the study, but it took a few months, even though I had sent my application by courier and had conducted several telephone conversations with the access officer.

There are endless possibilities for obtaining government files under the Privacy Act and Access to Information Act, although you may encounter snags. You might even find, as have some researchers, that some documents are more complete in English than in French! I recommend reading an excellent guide, *Using the Access to Information Act*, written by two lawyers, Heather Mitchell and Murray Rankin, and published in 1984 by International Self-Counsel Press. The book is written in plain English and, at 135 pages, is a quick, enjoyable read—well worth the $5.95 price tag.

Unravelling Court Records

Chapter Eighteen

Court record searches can be both a researcher's dream and a researcher's nightmare. A crucial advantage to such searches is that a court record may contain confidential information on individuals or businesses that is not available anywhere else. The problem is that access to these records is a great uncertainty and varies considerably from court to court. Some courts won't even allow you to sit in on civil or criminal proceedings, or examine the most basic documents, unless you're an involved party. Other courts allow you to attend legal proceedings and examine documents.

It's a good idea right from the start to consult with either the local court Registrar or the Clerk of the court to establish the court's policy. For a list of court offices across Canada, refer to the *Canadian Law List*. This is an annual publication available at many libraries.

If you are denied access to court proceedings or records, you may have to rely on one of the lawyers involved to obtain the information for you or, as a last resort, you may have to go to court to force the government to give you access.

It is unlikely, however, that you would have to use court records on more than the odd occasion. In fact, I can think of only two instances where court records gave me information that might not otherwise have been available.

As a journalist, I once wanted to know if the giant shoe manufacturer, Bata Industries Limited, was involved in the production of tank equipment for the United States Army. Interviews with various Bata officials, including Thomas Bata himself, didn't answer my question. However, an obscure court record, an affidavit filed by a senior Bata executive to obtain an injunction against picketing strikers, revealed that the company was indeed heavily involved in the defence industry.

On another occasion I required financial information on a privately owned, international soap company. I also needed background information on one of the firm's executives. By accessing this person's divorce records, I was able to glean both types of usually confidential information.

Despite the seemingly complex court network in Canada, I was able to locate the court records in both cases, because I understood the basic structure and jurisdictions of the courts and knew the types of documents that existed. Without this overview, my job would have been like searching for a needle in a haystack.

A word of caution: Avoid "fishing expeditions" with the staff at a court. If you show up at a county court and ask for assistance before you've narrowed down your request, don't expect much help. Here is an example of a vague request: "My father was involved in some sort of legal action in western Canada in the last few decades. Where can I find his files?"

You would stand a far better chance of accessing court records with a request like this: "My father, Sam J. Orez, was divorced in Toronto in 1979. Where can I find the court records for this divorce?"

This latter question is much more refined and therefore far easier to answer. The local litigation clerk or registrar should gladly assist you with such a question. The question pertains to a *civil* proceeding involving a divorce, which means that the records would be kept at the Supreme Court office for the judicial district of York. With the date of the divorce and the name of one of the parties involved, it is possible to pull the file for this case.

In other words, the secret to unravelling court records is to focus on the proper nature of the case, the jurisdiction of the court, and, eventually, the particular document you need.

Structure and
Jurisdiction

The first chapter of Clare Beckton's book, *The Law and the Media*, gave me a good overview of the structure of Canadian courts. There are two levels of courts in Canada—federal and provincial. The Supreme

Court of Canada is the country's final court of appeal for criminal and civil cases. In addition, there is the Federal Court, with a trial division (where cases are heard) and an appeal division. The Federal Court is responsible for such areas of law as immigration, citizenship, and taxation. Under the Constitution Act, 1867, provinces are vested with the power to establish their own courts. The names of these courts vary in different provinces, but their structure is essentially the same.

In order to begin searching for a court record, you must first understand if the case was a *civil* or *criminal* proceeding.

Civil Courts   Civil cases involve breaches of the relationship between persons; the amount of money involved in a claim helps to determine which court hears the case. However, most civil cases are settled out of court, after an *examination for discovery* or *discoveries*—a pretrial meeting where both parties obtain details from each other to determine if they will proceed to trial.

The civil court structure is as follows:

- *Small Claims Courts* handle disputes involving $3,000 or less.
- *County Courts* or *District Courts* handle disputes up to $25,000.
- The provincial *Queen's Bench* or *Supreme Court* handles disputes involving large settlements, for example, in Ontario, settlements involving $25,000 or more. However, certain cases, such as libel, slander, and bankruptcy are automatically heard at this level.
- Any appeals from these courts can be heard by the various provincial courts of appeal.
- There is a variety of "specialty courts" in various provinces. These vary depending on the needs of a particular province. They can include *Family Courts*, which hear cases involving juveniles and families, and *Surrogate* or *Probate Courts*, which handle the administration of wills and estates.

Criminal Courts   Criminal cases involve crimes against society or individuals, and these crimes are described in various federal and provincial statutes. A key piece of legislation is the *Criminal Code of Canada*, under which there are *summary convictions* (which involve less serious crimes, such as theft under $200) and *indictable offences* (which involve the most serious offences, such as rape and murder).

The nature of the crime determines which level of court hears a criminal proceeding. Criminal laws are administered through the provinces at any one of these levels of court:

- The *Provincial Court* or *Magistrates Court* hears most criminal cases—all summary convictions as well as some indictable offences.

  In the case of certain crimes, such as armed robbery, the accused has the right to choose to be tried at the Provincial Court level or at either of the higher courts—the County Court or Supreme Court. If the accused chooses a higher court, he or she may undergo a *preliminary hearing* at the Provincial Court level to determine if there is enough evidence to proceed to trial. The accused can also waive a preliminary hearing by admitting in court that there is sufficient evidence to make a committal.

  If an individual is accused of a more serious crime, such as murder, he or she is automatically tried by a higher court.
- *County Courts* or *District Courts* hear criminal matters such as drug trafficking, arson, burglary, and criminal negligence. Appeals from summary conviction may also be heard here. This level of criminal court is sometimes referred to as a *Superior Court.*
- The provincial *Queen's Bench* or *Supreme Court* (trial division) is the highest level of court for criminal trials in each province. It hears the most serious crimes and, through its appeal division, also hears appeals from the lower courts. It is known in some provinces as a *Superior Court.*

Identifying
Documents

With some understanding of the structure and jurisdiction of Canadian courts, you can determine the most logical place for records to be kept. You should also be aware of what types of documents exist, in order to restrict your search to those that can answer your questions. In this section a sampling of the key civil and criminal documents is provided.

Keep in mind that if a legal proceeding has been *completed*, most of the documents concerning it are contained in one file or in a batch of files kept in one courthouse. Also, older records are kept in various storage facilities; ask the staff in charge of records where they are located and how to access them.

If you intend to use any documents for publication purposes, be careful—another party may have made an application for an order restraining publication. Journalists beware: *Make sure that no such order exists before publishing any court records.* If you ignore such an order, you may be subject to contempt of court or libel proceedings.

The documents discussed below are common to most provinces, although some variations may be found in Quebec. Ask the staff in charge of records at the court concerned to clarify the name and contents of the documents you seek.

Also look for the forthcoming book being prepared for the Canadian Bar Foundation by Harold Levy, Deputy Secretary of the Law Reform Commission of Canada. It is expected to be released in the fall of 1985.

Civil Documents   ₋To access records from a civil case, begin with the name of one of the parties involved. (In legal jargon this is known as the *style of cause*.) Using a name, you can search through the annual Matters Index Books (usually kept near the main counter of the court office that stores legal records) for a *writ number* or a *statement of claim number*. (In some provinces, such as Ontario, writs are no longer issued. Instead, a statement of claim is used.) Civil court records in Canada are filed under one of these two reference numbering systems.

Cases are filed in the Matters Index Books by the surname of the person suing, followed by the surname of the person being sued. (Different courts label the parties differently—as the plaintiff versus the defendant, applicant versus respondent, or petitioner versus respondent.) It is therefore easier to use these alphabetically organized annual indexes if you have the plaintiff's name. But even with the defendant's name you can still find the reference number, although your search will take longer.

Once you have the reference number, simply approach the front counter of the courthouse and ask to see the appropriate files, which you can view on the premises. There isn't normally a fee to examine most court records, although there are photocopying charges.

The following are the main types of documents you can expect to find in a court file:

- A *statement of claim* is filed in court to initiate legal action, and it outlines precisely what the aggrieved person is claiming. Various counterclaims may be registered as well. And don't accept a statement of claim at face value: Always follow through on the case by checking to see what the final judgment, ruling, or court order was.

- A *statement of defence* is a written reply to the statement of claim.
- A *writ of summons* is issued to the person being sued. It states the damages incurred, what compensation is being sought, and gives the name and address of the person being sued.
- The *discovery of documents* is a meeting where both parties provide each other with pertinent documents to the case. These can include a broad range of materials, such as invoices, letters, and insurance agreements. Once these are submitted to the examination for discovery, they may or may not be declared as *exhibits*.
- An *examination for discovery* is a meeting where both parties cross-examine each other and present evidence and counterevidence to determine if the case should proceed to pretrial and trial. If one of the lawyers involved in the case requests and pays for a copy of the minutes of this meeting from the court, a copy will also be provided in the public file.
- A *pretrial* is held after the examination for discovery to try to settle the matter out of court. If a settlement is made, and one of the parties has requested the *minutes of settlement*, these minutes are filed in court as well. They outline what the precise settlement was. If there was an order made by a judge, that order is also recorded.
- *Motions* of various kinds may be heard by legal tribunals before a trial takes place. A motion may, for example, include adding parties and amending the pleadings, and it is heard before a *master* at *master's court*. A master doesn't have the full authority of a judge, and these decisions may be overturned. The master files a *master's report* outlining the judgment on a motion.

  Other kinds of motions, such as various forms of injunctions, are heard before a judge at *motions court* (sometimes called a *weekly court*). Records of any *interim orders* made are kept on file. You may also find various affidavits (sworn statements), judgments, and rulings on motions in the file.

  If you want to know only the outcome of a motion, look for the *motion record*. On the back of this document is a handwritten endorsement or denial of the motion by either a master or a judge.
- *Minutes of the trial* are generally prepared, along with affidavits, and these are generally available.

- *Judgments, orders,* and *endorsements* are recorded and filed. You may find that some courthouses keep judgments separately on microfilm, not in the general file.
- A *writ of execution (writ of seizure and sale* in Ontario) is an extremely useful post-court document. You can find this document in the general file or through the sheriff at the County or District Court office. A writ of execution flows from a court judgment and empowers the sheriff to seize and sell assets of a debtor, including real and personal property, because the individual has defaulted on payments.

  With a name and approximate date, you can search for this document at the sheriff's office. You can also obtain an abstract of the court judgment there. However, to access the full file, look for the court records in the court where the case was heard.

  A writ of execution does not state if the person has paid what the court has ordered, but it does indicate to a prospective buyer that there is a registered judgment against some of his or her real or personal property.
- *Last wills and testaments* are filed in Surrogate Court, a division of the County Court. With a name and approximate date, you can obtain a copy of a will.

Criminal Records   Criminal records are always more difficult to obtain than records of civil cases, and in most instances you have to give the court clerical staff a valid reason for examining them. (There is, however, no hard-and-fast rule about what constitutes a valid reason.) In nearly every instance you require some significant identifying features of the case, such as the full name of the accused, the date of the court proceeding, the level of court, and its geographical location.

If you do not have such details, you may be able to find them in newspaper accounts or from one of the lawyers involved in the case. If a judgment was rendered, you can search through the *Weekly Criminal Bulletin*, published by the Canada Law Book Incorporated. This publication gives an abstract of many criminal cases, including identifying pieces of information. (There is also an equivalent publication for civil cases, the *All-Canada Weekly Summaries*. Most libraries keep both of these.)

If you have enough information to identify a case to the staff at the court involved and need only to check the disposition of the legal proceeding, telephone the court directly. It is easier to obtain this information by telephone than it is to actually see the documents described below:

- The *information* is the document in which the accused is charged. It includes the name of the accused, age, address, and sometimes occupation.
- The *indictment* is another charging document, containing the same information. Once a person is committed to trial following a preliminary hearing, an indictment is prepared and serves as the basis for further proceedings.
- A *search warrant* is the document giving law enforcement officials the legal right to search a specific premise and to seize specific things.
- The *information to obtain a search warrant* is much more revealing than the search warrant itself. It includes an affidavit by the police officer involved, explaining why the police department believes a crime is being committed and how the warrant will help solve the crime. A Supreme Court of Canada ruling has made this document public information if the police have in fact seized what they set out to seize.

  Unfortunately, there is no central depository for this information, but generally it is kept at the Provincial Court. Ask the court staff for assistance in locating this document.
- The *transcript of a preliminary hearing* can also be revealing. A preliminary hearing takes place before a judge of a Provincial Court to determine whether there is sufficient evidence to proceed to trial. The transcript can be ordered from the court reporter, and this can be an expensive undertaking. You may, however, be able to borrow a copy of the transcript from one of the lawyers involved in the case.
- A *transcript of the trial* is available whenever a case goes to trial and may include testimonies of any witnesses. Again, you may have to pay a court reporter to transcribe a copy for you.
- *Exhibits* are usually filed in court as evidence of a person's innocence or guilt. Exhibits are physical evidence in any number of forms, from fingerprints on a glass to furniture. Exhibits are generally returned to their owners shortly after a court action has been completed, but some exhibits may be kept in a court file or in storage. Ask the court staff if they have any exhibits in storage.
- *Judgments*, *rulings*, and *orders* are crucial documents that state the final disposition of a case unless the decision is appealed. Judg-

ments may be included in a general court file along with other court documents, but sometimes they are kept separately on microfilm. Ask the court staff about this.

- *Appeals on judgments* are sometimes made, and the results of the appeal are recorded in a document.
- *Bail hearings* are held to determine if the accused can be released from jail, and under what conditions. The minutes of the proceedings may be filed if someone orders a transcript.
- *Bail Order Release Papers* are issued when the accused is released from custody. The release papers state any conditions or restrictions that may be attached to the release, such as a surety or recognizance. For example, the accused may not be allowed to go near a particular person or place. If an accused is released into the custody of another person, that person's name and address are stated in the document.
- *Presentence reports* are prepared by probation services to help determine the appropriate sentence for the accused. These documents are extremely difficult to obtain unless you are one of the solicitors involved in the case.
- *Motions* of various kinds can be introduced at different times during the litigation process. For example, if there is a lot of adverse publicity before a trial, the lawyer of the accused might file a motion for a change of venue in an attempt to have the trial moved to another location.

  To establish the outcome of a motion, look on the back of the *motion record*, where you will find a judge's handwritten endorsement or denial of the motion.

For additional information on criminal court matters, I recommend *Criminal Procedure in Canada* by P. Michael Bolton, published by International Self-Counsel Press.

BIBLIOGRAPHY

The following is a list of reference materials that I have acquired in an eclectic manner over the years; I have included a personal assessment of some of them. They have been used to meet my own information needs and are not a definitive list of reference sources, but they do show the range of materials available.

Business

The Blue Book of Canadian Business is published each year by Canadian Newspaper Services International, Toronto. Contains 106 in-depth profiles of major businesses and brief information on another 2,400 companies.

The Business Page by Wayne Cheveldayoff was published by Deneau, Ottawa, in 1980. A good overview of Canada's economy. 334 pages.

Canadian Business Corporations Act and Regulations, published annually by Richard De Boo, Don Mills, Ontario, explains how the act works and provides all the forms that businesses must complete. 254 pages.

Canadian Key Business Directory, in two volumes, provides profiles of 14,000 top Canadian businesses. Published annually by Dun and Bradstreet Canada, Toronto.

Canadian Mines Handbook and *Canadian Oil and Gas Handbook*, published each year by the Toronto-based Northern Miner Press, include company information on businesses involved in these industries.

Canadian Oil Register, published annually by Southam Communications, Don Mills, Ontario, lists 4,000 companies and over 15,000 key personnel in the oil industry.

Canadian Trade Index, published annually by the Toronto-based Canadian Manufacturers' Association, provides a useful survey of Canada's manufacturers that have more than a local distribution of products.

The *Card Index* is one of many useful services offered by the *Financial Post*'s Corporation Service Group of Maclean Hunter, Toronto. In-depth profiles of more than 600 publicly owned Canadian companies on handy index cards. Updated regularly.

A Dictionary of Canadian Economics by David Crane was published by Hurtig, Edmonton, in 1980. 372 pages.

Directory of Canadian Chartered Accountants is published annually by the Toronto-based Canadian Institute of Chartered Accountants.

Directory of Directors is published each year by the *Financial Post*, a division of Maclean Hunter. Lists key Canadian business people and their backgrounds. Very useful for anyone wanting to research interlocking directorships.

F & S Index International Annual is published each year by Predicasts, Cleveland, OH. Indexes over 750 business publications, newspapers, and reports on companies, products, and industries around the world.

The Financial Analysts Federation Membership Directory is published once a year by the Financial Analysts Federation, New York, NY. Includes Canadian members in some major cities. 397 pages.

Fraser's Canadian Trade Directory is published annually by Maclean Hunter in three volumes. An exhaustive list of Canadian businesses and industries with addresses, trade names, and foreign representatives.

How to Find Information about Companies by Washington Researchers is updated periodically. A do-it-yourself guide to researching private and public companies in the United States only available through Washington Researchers, 918 16th Street N.W., Washington, DC 20006. Their phone number is (202) 833-2230. Although it is an American publication, it can help researchers obtain information on Canadian companies operating in the U.S. Contains a handy list of companies that will obtain documents for you for a fee. 333 pages.

How to Incorporate a Small Business by Mel Montgomery was published in 1983 by Practical Small Business Publications, Vancouver. Everything you need to know about small businesses in British Columbia. 123 pages.

How to Invest in Canadian Securities was published in 1978 by the Toronto-based Canadian Securities Institute, the educational organization of the Canadian securities industry. Recommended reading to understand how public companies raise money. 339 pages.

"How to Snoop on Your Competitors," by Steven Flax, *Fortune*, May 1984, pages 29 to 33.

Inter-Corporate Ownership is published by Statistics Canada, Ottawa, every couple of years. Reveals the degree of foreign ownership and the corporate structure of companies operating in Canada. 1,062 pages.

Investment Terms and Definitions was published by the Canadian Securities Institute in 1973 and revised in 1981. 55 pages.

Moody's Investors Service, a company of the Dun and Bradstreet Corporation, Jersey City, NJ, publishes six major manuals each year that profile more than 20,000 businesses and corporations world-wide. Includes financial information on each.

Ontario Securities Act and Regulations with Policy Statements is printed annually by Richard De Boo. Good source for understanding the kinds of information public companies must file in Ontario. 549 pages.

The Ontario Securities Commission OSC Bulletin is published weekly by Dataline Incorporated, Toronto. An abbreviated list of all documents filed with the Ontario Securities Commission.

Researching Canadian Corporations by Manuel Gordon was published in 1977 by New Hogtown Press, Toronto. A very elementary list of sources of information that can be used to research businesses in Canada. 74 pages.

Scott's Industrial Directories contain a wealth of information on manufacturers across Canada. There are seven different directories in the series. Published by Southam Communications about every two years.

Sources of Information for Canadian Business by Brian Land is required reading for anyone doing serious research on business matters. Has been published by the Canadian Chamber of Commerce, Toronto, irregularly since 1962. The latest edition was published in 1978 and is still the best of its kind in Canada—I hope it will be revised. Contains a bibliography of sources of information on business matters. If you purchase only one book, let this be the one.

Survey of Industrials, Survey of Mines and Energy Resources, and *Survey of Predecessor and Defunct Companies* are three excellent directories published annually by Maclean Hunter. Contain a great deal of information on publicly owned Canadian corporations, including those that are no longer active.

Who Owns Whom in North America is published annually by Dun and Bradstreet and shows structure of companies, including a list of subsidiaries and associated companies. Other similar books published by Dun and Bradstreet include information on businesses in the United Kingdom and the Republic of Ireland.

Government

Annual Report of the Provincial Auditor of Ontario is printed annually by the Queen's Printer, Toronto. Each province has an equivalent publication summarizing the findings of the provincial auditor's audit of the public accounts. Information on the spending practices of the provincial government, any improper administrative and accounting procedures, and recommendations for futher government efficiency. Generally available from provincial government bookstores.

Canadian News Facts provides a synopsis of important news items, including information on the federal government. Published weekly in loose-leaf form by Marpep Publishing, Toronto.

The Corpus Administrative Index is published annually, along with its subject guide, by Southam Communications, Don Mills, Ontario. Lists key personnel of provincial and federal governments and their telephone numbers.

Data Users Directory: Who to Dial at Statistics Canada is an extremely useful directory for anyone requiring statistical information. Lists key department heads at Statistics Canada. Published twice a year by Statistics Canada, Ottawa, and available from their local offices free of charge.

Government of Canada Telephone Directory National Capital Region is published twice a year by the Department of Communications Government Telecommunications Agency and is available from the Canadian Government Publishing Centre, Ottawa, or from local bookstores designated as official bookstore agents. (Five other volumes for the Ontario, Pacific, Atlantic, Prairie, and Quebec regions are published annually. These six telephone books contain every federal government telephone number across the country.)

How Ottawa Spends, edited by Allan M. Maslove, is published annually by Methuen Publications, Agincourt, Ontario, and takes a hard look at the federal government's spending policies.

Index to Federal Programs and Services is published annually by the Canadian Government Publishing Centre. Includes information on 131 federal departments, agencies, and Crown corporations, and addresses and telephone numbers of federal government offices across Canada. Highly recommended. 550 pages.

Information U.S.A. by Matthew Lesko was published by Penguin Books, New York, NY, in 1983. The most comprehensive book I know on how to access any kind of information from the U.S. government. 990 pages.

Microlog is an index of reports from all levels of government and institutional sources. Published monthly by Micromedia Limited, Toronto, with a cumulative index at the end of each year.

Ottawa Letter is published weekly by CCH Canadian Limited, Toronto. A wide assortment of useful information on what is happening behind the scenes in the federal government.

Personal Information Index is published by the federal Minister of Supply and Services, Ottawa. Describes the personal information under the control of the federal government. Useful for anyone who wants to find out what information the federal government keeps on them. Most major post offices and libraries keep a copy.

Provincial Pulse is published twice a month by CCH Canadian and reports the news from all provincial legislatures and government departments. The publisher also produces a broad range of other reference materials of great value to anyone involved in the labour movement or with legal issues.

The Public Accounts of Canada is published annually by the Receiver General for Canada and is available through the Canadian Government Publishing Centre. In three volumes, it details the federal government's spending habits.

Public Accounts of Ontario is published annually by the Ontario Ministry of Treasury and Economics, Toronto, in three volumes. Outlines how provincial government money in Ontario is spent — from the salaries of civil servants to grants to private industry. Other provinces have similar books.

The Report of the Auditor General of Canada to the House of Commons is published by the Auditor General of Canada and is available from the Canadian Government Publishing Centre. Criticizes government spending where appropriate.

The Source Book: The Corpus Almanac is published annually by Southam Communications and contains a wealth of information on Canada, including government addresses and telephone numbers across the country. An excellent reference tool in two volumes.

Using the Access to Information Act was written by two gifted lawyers, Heather Mitchell and Murray Rankin, and published by International Self-Counsel Press, Vancouver, in 1984. If you plan to use freedom of information laws in this country, you must read this book. 135 pages.

You and Your Local Government by C. R. Tindal focusses on Ontario but is still an excellent primer on the ways in which local governments function. Published by the Ontario Municipal Management Development Board, Toronto, in 1982. 143 pages.

Labour

Collective Bargaining Information Sources is published by the Industrial Relations Information Service of Labour Canada, Ottawa. An invaluable reference guide to the many kinds of information available for collective bargaining and other industrial relations purposes in Canada. Lists practically every source in Canada with addresses and telephone numbers and updated regularly. Available free of charge to anyone involved in industrial relations.

Corporations and Labour Unions Returns Act is published annually by Statistics Canada, Ottawa, in two volumes. Includes a lot of useful data on national and international unions operating in Canada.

The Current Industrial Relations Scene in Canada, edited each year by W. D. Wood and Pradeep Kumar, is published by the Industrial Relations Centre, Queen's University, Kingston, Ontario. An important reference book for anyone involved in industrial relations. Provides analysis and statistics. 695 pages.

Directory of Labour Organizations in Canada is published each year by Labour Canada and provides information on national and international unions as well as independent labour organizations. A good guide for looking up addresses and acquiring quick statistics.

Law

The Canadian Law Dictionary, published by the Law and Business Publications (Canada), Toronto, in 1980, is a very useful source book for legal terms.

Canadian Law List is published annually by the Canada Law Book, Aurora, Ontario. A mammoth book listing the addresses of government and other sources relating to legal issues, including courts. 1,794 pages.

Courts and the Media by Stuart M. Robertson was published by Butterworths, Scarborough, Ontario, in 1981. An excellent book that unravels the court process in Canada. Chapter Four has been especially helpful to me by clarifying what access is allowed to some court records. 336 pages.

Criminal Procedure in Canada by P. Michael Bolton was published in its sixth edition in 1983 by International Self-Counsel Press, Vancouver. An excellent source book for understanding the criminal justice system in Canada. 152 pages.

The Justice System in Ontario was published by the Ontario Provincial Secretariat for Justice, Toronto. A simple overview of the court structure in Canada, focussing particularly on Ontario. May be obtained free of charge from the Secretariat or the Ontario Government Bookstore.

Latin Words and Phrases for Lawyers was published by Law and Business Publications (Canada) in 1980. Translations of significant Latin words, phrases, and maxims used by the legal profession. Very useful in interpreting legal documents. 335 pages.

The Law and the Media by Clare F. Beckton was published by The Carswell Company, Agincourt, Ontario, in 1982. The first chapter is an excellent overview of Canada's legal system and court structure. 161 pages.

The Lawyer's Desk Book is published annually by The Carswell Company and includes an excellent overview of the court system in Canada. Most of its contents focus on access to information in Ontario. 493 pages.

Research

Finding Facts Fast by Alden Todd was republished in 1979 by Ten Speed Press, Berkeley, CA, and is written for the American market. A brief list of ideas to keep in mind when using a library. 121 pages.

How to Win with Information or Lose without It by Andrew P. Garvin and Hubert Bermont was published by Bermont Books, Washington, DC, in 1980. If you're not sure of the value of information, this book is for you. Presents a sound philosophical argument about why information is crucial to making successful decisions. Also contains a good list of sources of business information available in the U.S. 170 pages.

A Legal Research Manual by Doug Macellven was published by Butterworths, Scarborough, Ontario, in 1983. A good overview of how to search for material with a legal bent. 316 pages.

The Reporter's Handbook: An Investigator's Guide to Documents and Techniques, edited by John Ullmann and Steve Honeyman, was published by St. Martin's Press, New York, NY, in 1983. Excellent for exploring techniques of research and sources available on a multitude of subjects in the U.S. 504 pages.

Research: A Practical Guide to Finding Information by Peter Fenner and Martha A. Armstrong was published by William Kaufmann, Los Altos, CA, in 1981. Good advice on how to use libraries to obtain information on science and technology. 174 pages.

Research Shortcuts by Judi Kesselman-Turkel and Franklynn Peterson was published by Contemporary Books, Chicago, IL, in 1982. A quick read that will tell you how to organize your thoughts and use a library. Written for first-year university students. 112 pages.

Where to Go for What: How to Research, Organize, and Present Your Ideas by Mara Miller was published by Prentice-Hall, Englewood Cliffs, NJ, in 1981. An extremely well-written and interesting book that explores the techniques of research. Worthwhile reading, even though the references are limited to American sources. 244 pages.

Winning by Telephone by Gary S. Goodman was published by Prentice-Hall Canada, Scarborough, Ontario, in 1982. Recommended reading if you want to learn how to use the telephone effectively. One of several books by Goodman on this subject. 144 pages.

Writer's Research Handbook by Keith M. Cottam and Robert W. Pelton was published in 1978 by Barnes and Noble, New York, NY. An introduction to American reference books. I do not recommend it to writers, although high school students would find it useful.

Tracing People

Catalogue of Directories Published and Areas Covered by Members of International Association of Cross Reference Directory Publishers. Despite the long title, this is a short book. Last published in 1983 and provides a good list of city directories across North America, along with their publishers' names and addresses. It doesn't list all city directories, but it still goes a long way. (City directories are compiled in a variety of ways and may contain a great deal of information on people, including occupation, address, how long the person has had a particular telephone number, and much more.) Published by Cole Publications, Lincoln, NE, 68521. 93 pages.

Tracing Your Ancestors in Canada, revised edition, 1983, Public Archives of Canada, Manuscript Division, Ottawa. Telephone (613) 995-5138. A do-it-yourself guide for tracing your family roots. Available free of charge. 37 pages.

Without a Trace, Partisan Press, P. O. Box 2193, Seattle, WA 98111, in 1980. It appears to have been written to teach anarchists how to avoid being traced by police. It summarizes all the major techniques police forces use to trace people — from blood samples to dirt traces — and explains how they are done. Fascinating reading. 125 pages.

General Reference

Amnesty International Report, published by Amnesty International Publications, London, England, appears every year and documents abuses of human rights around the world.

Association of Canadian Publishers is published annually by the Toronto-based Association of Canadian Publishers. Available free of charge. 47 pages.

Association of Consulting Engineers of Canada is published by that organization, based in Ottawa, on an ongoing basis. The two-volume set lists consulting engineers and their area of expertise.

Canada Year Book, published annually by the federal Minister of Supply and Services, Ottawa, provides a wide range of data on the economic, social, and political life of Canada.

Canadian Almanac and Directory, edited by Susan Bracken, is published annually by Copp Clark Pitman, Toronto. Includes names and addresses of key officials and departments at all levels of government, a long list of associations, and other useful information. 1,200 pages.

Canadian Business Index is published monthly by Micromedia Limited, Toronto, with a cumulative index at the end of each year. Includes about 200 major business publications in Canada. An invaluable tool.

The Canadian Encyclopedia will be published in three volumes for the first time by Hurtig, Edmonton, in 1985 and will contain over 2,000 pages of useful information on all aspects of Canada, including over 3,000 biographies. I have read some of the entries and recommend the encyclopedia to anyone interested in doing any kind of research in Canada.

Canadian Library Handbook is published each year by Micromedia and lists about 5,000 public, college, university, government, and special libraries in Canada. 230 pages.

The Canadian Market Place by Michael J. Trebilcock and Patricia McNeill was published by CBC Enterprises, Toronto, in 1983 to inform the public about their legal rights as consumers. 143 pages.

Canadian Medical Directory is published annually by Seccombe House, a division of Southam Communications, Don Mills, Ontario. Lists doctors by province and town as well as all hospitals in Canada.

Canadian News Index is published monthly by Micromedia with a cumulative index at the end of each year. Indexes seven of the country's major newspapers by subject and name. Invaluable for any researcher.

Canadian Reference Sources by Dorothy Ryder was published by the

Ottawa-based Canadian Library Association in 1981. The information is updated by "Canadian Reference Books; Or Benevolent Ignorance Dispelled" by Edith T. Jarvi and Diane Henderson, *Reference Services Review*, Volume 2, Fall 1983, pages 87 to 95 with bibliography.

Canadian Serials Directory was compiled by Martha Pluscauskas and published by University of Toronto Press, Toronto, 1977. An excellent and unique bibliographic tool, even though some of its listings are now dated. A good index of periodicals and serials, including some company newsletters, yearbooks, journals, proceedings, and transactions of associations and societies. Divided into three sections: alphabetical list of serials, subject, and publisher.

Canadian Who's Who, published annually by University of Toronto Press, profiles notable Canadians. About 1,184 pages.

Directory of Associations in Canada is edited by Brian Land and Diane Gallagher and published once a year by Micromedia. Invaluable for locating organizations or experts. Lists 8,000 associations, each of which is indexed under 800 subject classifications, and the serials of each association. 317 pages.

Directory of Survey Organizations was last published by Statistics Canada, Ottawa, in 1981. Lists hundreds of companies that provide custom research. The department plans an updated version in 1985.

Information Sources is published annually by the Information Industry Association, Washington, DC. It is the membership directory of that association and lists over 150 companies and their offices in countries around the world that provide various custom information services. 363 pages.

Omni Online Database Directory by Mike Edelhart and Owen Davies was published by Collier Macmillan, Don Mills, Ontario, in 1983. I hope it will be updated. Provides a list and description of over 1,000 data bases available to the public and a handy subject index. 292 pages.

Ulrich's International Periodicals Directory is published every two years by R. R. Bowker, New York, NY. (A quarterly publication, *Ulrich's Quarterly*, brings the *Directory* up-to-date.) Provides a list of all major publications and states which have been indexed and where. This saves a researcher a lot of unnecessary time wading through back issues of publications, because it alerts him or her to the fact that an index exists. (A similar publication is the *Standard Periodical Directory*.)

Who Knows What: Canadian Library-Related Expertise is compiled by award-winning librarian Susan Klement. A directory of librarians and other research specialists published by the Canadian Library Association on an ongoing basis. 174 pages.

INDEX

Credits

Grateful acknowledgment is made to the following business organizations and government departments for permission to reprint copyrighted material. Every effort has been made to trace copyright holders, and any errors or omissions drawn to the publisher's attention will be rectified in subsequent editions.

Tables 14.1, 14.2, 14.3, 14.4, and 14.5: Micromedia Limited, Toronto, Ontario.
Table 15.1: Department of Buildings & Inspections, City of Toronto.
Table 15.2: Committee of Adjustment, City of Toronto.
Tables 16.1 and 16.2: Ministry of Consumer and Commercial Relations. Reproduced by permission of the Deputy Minister of Government Services.
Table 17.1: Corporations Branch, Department of Consumer and Corporate Affairs. Reproduced by permission of the Minister of Supply and Services Canada.
Table 17.2: Statistics Canada.
Tables 17.3 and 17.4: Treasury Board. Reproduced by permission of the Minister of Supply and Services Canada.